Ukrainian Refugees
2022

Pavlo Pavliuk
Ukrainian Refugees 2022

All rights reserved
Copyright © 2025 by Pavlo Pavliuk

No part of this publication may be reproduced, distributed, or transmitted in any form or by any means, including photocopying, recording, or other electronic or mechanical methods, without the prior written permission of the publisher, except in the case of brief quotations embodied in critical reviews and certain other noncommercial uses permitted by copyright law.

—

Published by - Spines
ISBN: 979-8-89691-413-6

Ukrainian Refugees 2022

The story of THE Ukrainian Family

Pavlo Pavliuk

Contents

Foreword	7
To the Reader	9
1. The Beginning	13
2. Emergency suitcase	19
3. Decision Made	28
4. A Long Journey	32
5. Unexpected Road Hazards	37
6. Crossing the Border	44
7. Wonderful News	48
8. Where to Next?	55
9. Trying to Find Our Bearings	61
10. An Angel?	67
11. New Realities	72
12. Where Do We Go From Here?	77
13. A New Country?	86
14. Response	94
15. Saying Goodbye	96
16. A Surprise with the Airline Tickets	98
17. The Flight	102
18. So, when, finally?	109
19. A New Beginning	112
20. Is That for Real?	119

Foreword

The purpose of this book is to tell the world about over 6 million Ukrainian refugees, who since 2022, due to unforeseen circumstances, have found themselves far from home.

Perhaps no one can truly understand our pain and daily struggles better than ourselves, who share a similar journey one way or another.

Please do not remain silent. Share your incredible stories wherever you are, in any country of the world, where fate has led us. Let our stories become a source of inspiration, fueling daily victories of the people around us.

Our mission is to bring Ukraine's victory closer, each of us contributing in our own unique way, through our achievements and opportunities.

Together we are strong. Each of us is a warrior of light and a guardian of our homeland's well-being.

A portion of the proceeds from this book's sales will be directed toward supporting the Armed Forces of Ukraine.

To the Reader

I have often had to recount our family's story—a story that changed our lives forever, starting from the first day of the hostile russian invasion into Ukraine.

Since it turned out to be as gripping as a movie script, I decided to put it on paper. This way, I could preserve it in writing script instead of retelling it over and over again, as I've already done dozens of times. Why not offer a book for reading instead? Of course, storytelling will never truly end.

I wanted the book to be an easy, engaging read, written in a simple, conversational style. I intentionally kept it concise so it could be read in one sitting while still capturing the most essential moments.

I also included cultural highlights of the countries we visited, which left a strong impression on us. I detailed the emotions and experiences of Ukrainian refugees abroad, each of whom had their own unique and irreplaceable journey.

The writing style resembles a diary. Since I don't usually keep one, it was important to sit down, carefully recall everything, and document it before the details faded with time. I'm glad I made the effort, and I'll explain why. I would've loved to read about the lives and experiences of my own ancestors, their joys and struggles, about whom I know so little. I'm convinced their manuscripts would have been passed down through generations like family treasures!

Today, writing a book is much easier thanks to modern technologies, so I took advantage of that. I believe this was time well spent. I've already devoted a couple of months to writing this book, crafting it in both Ukrainian and English.

I encourage every reader to start writing their own life story. Why not? I am certain your life is no less captivating than ours. Future generations will be grateful for your efforts and memories!

Above all, I want to thank our God Jesus Christ for His constant presence in our lives, His love and protection.

I want to express my deepest gratitude to our dear parents: Oleksandr and Dina Pavliuk, Margarita Piskedda and others, who pray for us daily.

To my beloved wife Tanya and our children, David, Daniel, and Daniela, who are the central figures in this book. Thank

To the Reader

you David and Daniel for your assistance and encouragement!

My dear wife Tanya wasn't able to participate in writing of the book, wishing to erase these events from her memory forever, to let them sink into oblivion like a bad dream.

My love, I'm sorry I couldn't shield you from the circumstances that were beyond my control!

Unfortunately, revisiting these memories reopened old wounds, forcing us to relive events that left deep scars on our hearts.

Many of those wounds are still bleeding. Our story isn't over yet; it continues to unfold. Every day, bombs and missiles strike our homeland, killing and injuring our compatriots, and destroying our homes and infrastructure.

Special thanks and deep respect go to the Ukrainian soldiers who risk their lives and health daily for the welfare of our nation, proud to be called Ukraine. It's because of you, our heroes, that we can say with pride, We are Ukrainians!

I wake up at night praying to God to protect and keep you warm. It's January now, and I can't imagine how you endure the freezing trenches and dugouts. My deepest respect to your parents, wives, and children, who have let go of their loved ones, brave enough to defend our land.

Gratitude also goes to the president of Ukraine Volodymyr Oleksandrovych Zelensky, who took on the fight, like a lion brave to protect the sacred ground and sovereignty of our nation. Thank you for the thousands of hours spent negotiating with foreign partners at every level.

To the nations and governments of the United States of America, the European Union, Canada, Japan, South Korea, and others—sincere appreciation. It's impossible to name everyone individually, but we bow deeply to you all!

I want to specifically thank and recognize:

Oleksandr and Olga Levchenko,

Kees van Aalst, Jan and Liz van Aai, Arnold and Carola van Dorp,

Marten and Barbara Koopman,

Isabelle Joy, Daniel and Tami Stagg,

Roy and Cindy Brantley, Jerry Fox,

Rev. Brian Smith, Cody Blair, Jill and Jeremy Blest, Pavlo and Miron Havrilyuk

and many others, who worked tirelessly to protect us from the blows and trials of fate.

1. The Beginning

On the cold winter morning of Thursday, February 24, 2022, our day began.

It began and continues to this day.

We had no clue that very soon, our lives would be divided into BEFORE and AFTER.

It was just another ordinary night in our lives. The day's worries were winding down, and people were getting ready for bed.

Before sleep, our family usually gets together in one of the rooms of our house to share impressions of the day or speak up our prayer requests. Another day was about to slip into oblivion.

But this night would remain etched in our memories forever, leaving a deep scar in our history.

Some shared their joys, while others were seeking support or even miracles, which we had witnessed time and again in our lives. We pray and uplift each other. This tradition continues to this day.

It's rare for us to get to bed early! This night was no exception. Once again, we stayed up late, waiting for the moon to rise.

So much was happening around us that day, and we felt somewhat worried and unsure.

My beloved wife, Tanya, had a gut feeling that something was about to happen, and it made her uneasy. Even our German shepherd, Elsa, was restless that night.

Everyone was talking about the russians, who had been stationed on our border for quite a while, forming a combat force and preparing for an invasion, collecting donor blood for their armed forces.

The day before, all the foreign embassies we knew of had either been evacuated or were preparing for evacuation. Foreign citizens were leaving our country as well, following the advice of their embassies.

With the words, "God is in control" and "Let His will be done", we finally went to our rooms. It was already very late, and the kids needed to wake up early for school, while Tanya and I had to go to work.

Two of our children were students at the local school. Our eldest son was attending college. Tanya worked as an English teacher at a private school.

Once I witnessed how her students greeted her at the school gates. They met her even before she reached the gates!

Everyone wanted to hug her and exchanged embraces with her in return. It was an honor for them to help her carry her heavy teacher's bag filled with textbooks!

Tanya wasn't just a teacher but a gifted educator who loved her job and achieved excellent results in her teaching.

The children felt her genuine care and expressed their gratitude in return.

I worked at a newly built construction materials supermarket in the city of Zhytomyr.

There was a reason for that.

As an interpreter, I had a hard time finding work starting from my city on. My clients, due to safety concerns, chose not to take any risks by coming to Ukraine anymore.

The first loss of clients happened back in 2014 when the hostile country began preparing for its large-scale invasion in various directions, starting with the Crimean Peninsula and Eastern Ukraine, spreading propaganda among the people living in those areas.

The second loss of clients came with the onset of COVID when even those groups that had been visiting Ukraine annually for the last twenty years canceled their trips for the first time.

It was a quiet and peaceful winter night outside.

Suddenly, at five in the morning, the earth shook.

The silence of the night was shattered by a deafening explosion near our house.

It felt as though someone's gas heater had exploded or something of that nature. It was the winter season, after all.

Could one of the neighbors have had a heating system failure? We felt so sorry for them. Hopefully everyone is alive.

All the dogs on our street started barking loudly and were scared. We were all just as scared!

It's been pitch dark outside. What in the world is going on in here? Our sleepy heads couldn't make out anything.

The explosion and shaking of the ground were so strong that our daughter, Daniela, whose room was on the second floor of the house, almost fell out of her bed, as she later confessed.

We noticed two cracks appeared inside of the three-layer glass of our front door, looking like lightning bolts.

Later on, we learned that the residents of the buildings near the epicenter of the explosion reported that all their windows and glass doors shattered into fragments, just like the windshield of a car! The shockwave had flown into the rooms where people were peacefully sleeping, injuring many of them.

There were no news reports yet due to the early hour. We couldn't find any information online either. I tried to go back to bed and fall asleep again, knowing that in one hour I would have to wake up and get ready for work.

As dawn just began to break, Tanya noticed a column of black smoke rising like a chimney from behind the forest, where a military airfield was located.

Later, we learned that a russian bomber had struck a fuel tank with a missile, targeting the military infrastructure of the airfield.

I have hard time believing that in 2022, in the heart of Europe could break out a war!

For a better word to use in this circumstance would be a genocide. That's right. A genocide. A genocide of the Ukrainian nation right in front of the eyes of the entire world!

It was crystal clear from the fact that, as soon as the

invaders were capturing towns and villages, the first thing they did was penetrate the local school library and set the books on fire!

They hated the Ukrainian language to such an extent! Even more, they hated people who speak it.

Right after the arson, the invaders bring in "knowledgeable" russian teachers to the occupied areas, where every morning the Ukrainian children are forced to listen to the anthem of the terrorist state, deeply instilling propaganda into the minds of the little ones starting from a young age.

One of the terrorists killed in action had a message written on his bulletproof vest: "Speak russian or die."

I was so convinced of my belief in a peaceful resolution that I lost a bet to my wife: a large cake! I was that certain that a full-scale invasion would be prevented, being convinced that somehow everything would be fixed. Through diplomacy or some other way, everything should surely be settled!

No one even considered the fact that the hostile federation had been secretly and audaciously preparing to seize territories of independent countries for the past twenty years. That was a reason why they were not willing to negotiate anything with anybody. They had a plan.

For some reason, they decided to start implementing their insidious plan with Ukraine, mistakenly thinking it would be easy prey.

In their demonic plans, the invaders aimed to capture Ukraine in just three days. What a bunch of hopeless failures!

The enemies had full access to state secrets and military objects during the pro-russian presidency of traitor Viktor

Yanukovych, who now lives in the capital of an unfriendly country. He granted russians unhindered access to any objects they wished, deliberately destroying Ukraine's Armed Forces and aiding the enemy.

It was the reason they thought capturing new lands would be like a walk in the park.

In their sick dreams, they planned to capture Ukraine in three days.

Now three years have already passed by. Those pathetic losers are still working hard nowadays on their shabby plan. Three long years in a row they've been receiving the punishment they deserve, thanks to the heroic resistance of the Ukrainian people and the bravery of Ukraine's Armed Forces!

Who would have thought that Ukrainians had to pay such an enormous price for their freedom?

For the right to live peacefully in its towns and villages, tilting the soil of their prominent ancestors and raising kids on their own land!

2. Emergency suitcase

Few words about our family.

Our first son's name is David, and he is seventeen years old.

Daniel, age thirteen.

Daniela, our daughter, was seven.

All of their names start with the letter "D," which adds up to 3D, making our world three-dimensional!

My wife and I shared the same last name, Pavliuk, before we got married.

On top of that, three years later, David was born exactly on our wedding day, May 27th!

Our history teachers taught us in school that since the founding of the United Nations, there would be no more wars because countries had agreed to recognize the borders and territorial integrity of one another.

Yet, a permanent member with veto power is committing genocide right in front of the eyes of the entire world, which is watching it daily. They dare to break every international principle with impunity!

The horrors of the Second World War, witnessed by our ancestors, should never be repeated. We really did believe that.

It is painful to realize that our unfortunate neighboring country doesn't share the same values, and history still hasn't taught them anything yet.

That's a shame.

They do not realize that, besides it all, there is God who watches over everything they do!

Many believers from many countries these days asking God day and night to reveal His justice to those who give bloodshed orders and carry them out, or those who support so-called "russian peace" policy would share same responsibility for committing crimes against humanity daily three years long now.

It will never be forgotten. Never.

Surpassing the crimes of the Nazis in the Second World War, whose atrocities we now learn about from films and books based on real events, the russian invaders in 2022 breached the border of a sovereign European country and started killing civilians of all ages on their way with no remorse.

Acting worse than the Mongol-Tatars of the distant past, their behavior resembled that of recent Hamas terrorists invasions into Israel- an avalanche, destroying everything in their path!

It looked like if the gates of hell had opened wide and the demons of evil were unleashed!

In the initial moments of the attack, our people did not expect such cruelty.

In the understanding of a mentally healthy person, war takes place in some battlefield vicinities. Soldiers fight against each other while being in relatively equal conditions, like boxers in a ring.

Our women that dreadful morning were calmly walking with their babies in strollers. Children were peacefully heading to school, thinking about their studies and lessons.

These shameful monsters from the pit with human appearance, began attacking and raping our women, girls, and even infants! Weapons fell into the hands of scoundrels, and humanity suddenly disappeared.

Weapons fell into the hands of scoundrels, and humanity suddenly disappeared.

Or rather, it had never been there.

Many of the invaders have relatives living in Ukraine. They occasionally visited them from time to time and knew their neighbors and friends. Perhaps they were meeting those people now on their way and shooting them!

They shot a man who was peacefully riding his bicycle between two villages. When he was discovered, he was lying beside his bicycle, obviously unaware that he would be shot at. It had been done either for fun or for reasons known only to them!

These fiends shot homeowners at point-blank range, looted their houses, and loaded their trucks with stolen goods from murdered Ukrainians under the symbol of the swastika, the letters "V" or "Z", and, via Belarus, their close allies, were mailing the stolen items to their unknown worlds.

The occupiers' actions reminded us of the Bolsheviks during Soviet times, who were sent to forcibly rob Ukraine from the very same kremlin that governs today.

Taking grain and crops from starving Ukrainians in the years 1927-1933, those russian rascals deliberately left entire families to starve to death. Around 15,000,000 Ukrainians starved to death in those three artificial famines!

They starved Ukrainians for their refusal to join their "Collective Farm" system. By that time Ukraine was known as " The Bread Basket of Europe"!

The Soviets wanted to "teach" Ukrainians how to maintain the land.

Did they realize that growing crops is the genes of Ukrainians inherited from our gallant ancestors? They simply wanted to use up my country to feed that newly created formation of countries, called Soviet Union, under Moscow dictatorship.

They were historically highly interested in capturing our land by any cost. They had even stolen the name of our land!

Historically Ukraine was called the Kievan Rus. They were called Muscovy.

Back in the day their land was famous for numerous swamps and mire, swarming with mosquitoes and wild ducks, natural inhabitants of that area. Muscovy ducks can have some disadvantages, including their tendency to compete with native species, damage property, and their gluttonous appetite.

They are known for their red facial skin and bright red caruncles around their eyes and beak.

What color was preferred for the Soviet flag I wonder?

They needed our prominent deep-rooted history to use as a foundation for the newly made-up formation consisting of the conquered countries.

Because without historical roots you are next to nothing.

Some of the remains of the ghostly-looking barns are still standing in the Ukrainian fields, resembling concentration camps, serve as monuments to the incompetence of their disastrous government.

While Ukraine finally commenced implementing the long awaited decommunization reforms, started right after the Orange Revolution, such as renaming the streets, demolishing Lenin statues and attach importance to the Ukrainian language as a national language- immediately it became intolerable for our arch enemy, our Northern greedy neighbour, who presently owns 1/6 of the dry land!

Just think of that. These russian soldiers are the children and grandchildren of those notorious forebears from the past!

With the same mindset to conquer and enslave Ukraine. Nothing has been really changed at all.

A good number of the russian soldiers came here from such remotest places that they had never seen a toilet in their lives. They were taking water from them to drink!

After figuring out what they were meant for, they dismantled and loaded those into their "Z" and "V" marked military vehicles to mail them home all to make their families happy.

One old man complained that they took all his used underwear and worn socks!

Surveillance cameras captured them in offices, where they were curiously inspecting office equipment. It looked like they were seeing it for the first time. Their "advanced faces" definitely displayed genuine interest in something they hardly seen ever before.

One of them asked an office worker, "What is that thing hanging there on the wall?"

The worker replied, "It's a modem."

"What does it do?" asked the russian intellectual. "It provides internet connection," the office worker answered, having to explain it all to an individual with a machine gun.

After thinking for a moment, the russian soldier ripped it off the wall, saying that he would hook it up to the electricity and finally have internet in his house!

Can you even fathom the profound depth of intelligence of the russian soldier?

They were killing our children, looted their toys then mailing those to their own children, as was repeatedly recorded by surveillance cameras.

They stripped jewelry from the bodies of our women and girls to please their wives and daughters for allowing their husbands and daddies to take part in so-called in their terminology "special military operation."

One of the invaders was captured in a photo transporting looted goods, toilets, washing machines and a doghouse on his military truck with the swastika "Z " symbol!

Numerous trucks after capture by Ukrainian military

were filled up to the top with household appliances and utensils of the murdered Ukrainian households.

Once I come across photos of dozens of wrecked luxury sports cars near the Ukrainian capital. All of them had the "signature brand" of a "valiant russian soldier" from the terrorist country.

Like a maniac he was leaving a mark behind, an axe stuck in the hood of expensive foreign cars.

No single mentally balanced person could never ever be able to understand this. Let's say one had never seen a luxury sports car in his life. Why not have a ride on a stolen car? Feel it power and speed. Why destroy it with an axe, breaking its windows and damaging the body and engine with the axe!

What is inside of their heads I wonder?

The same crime was committed by the occupiers against the largest Ukrainian-made cargo plane, the biggest in the world in its class, called Mriya (a Dream), serving as a single prototype. They burned it to the ground!

One of the many towns and villages that suffered tremendously from the russian horde was the town of Bucha.

This place is located in a picturesque area in the middle of a forest near the capital of Ukraine, forty minutes away from our house, was damaged beyond belief.

Except for me, my family started organising so-called "emergency suitcases." Following a checklist, they packed the essentials into their backpacks or suitcases.

Later, survival experts on television, began advising people to have such bags prepared and ready. Just in case. You would also find plenty of helpful information in the internet about how to do it right.

While my family was working on it, I still couldn't take the whole story seriously being incredibly upset for not being able to answer my simple questions.

How can someone pack his entire life into a single suitcase?

Can the dream house, we had spent the last eight years building, suddenly lift off and float through space, just like in that cartoon where the house was tied to balloons?

What about our five beloved cats with their unique leopard-like markings, who loved basking in The Sun on our windowsills?

And our three dogs. What were we supposed to do with them all? Maybe we could take with us our Elsa, the black-and-tan long-haired German shepherd? Could we also fit our other two dogs, Julia and Bagheera, into the suitcase as well? How would that even look?

Maybe we could dismantle all the elements of our house, the ones we had so passionately chosen over those long eight years, and pack them into a suitcase too?

What about our forty young trees, which had just begun bearing fruit, standing tall, surrounded by wreath made of freshly trimmed grass around them. They grew gradually, gifting us with fruit each year and delighting our eyes. What suitcase could we fit them?

It feels like the house is on fire and one needs to get everything he wants in amount of just a few seconds of time!

Sometimes, at sunset, I'd step out onto the balcony, look around me and thank God for everything He gave us in our life to enjoy.

I thought it would always be like this! Once, I was an English translator, booked months, even a year in advance.

One group of foreigners would arrive at the airport while another was leaving.

This had been the rhythm of my life for nearly twenty years.

And now, even the U.S. Embassy has been evacuated.

A suitcase, you say.

What suitcase?

3. Decision Made

The windows of our house overlook the intercity highway, as we live about three kilometers away from the city line, in an area of new buildings around Zhytomyr.

Looking outside, it seemed to us that we had never seen such a busy highway before! With little distance in between, all kinds of vehicles were speeding up along the highway leaving the city.

Interesting enough. We were quite surprised to see that. Something very serious must be happening right now I thought to myself, in the same time looking for my boss's phone number. She would be greatly surprised to hear in a moment I'm not coming to work today. And that it is probably my last day in my position. I worked in the online delivery department of a hypermarket.

All my thoughts were consumed now with the trip.

A trip to nowhere.

Opening the garage gate, I looked at my iron friend with

much hope and expectation than ever before. Now I saw it as our means of rescue, like a lifebuoy.

"Good morning, Qashqai," I said.

I'm used to talking to everything as if it were alive. I speak to trees, to animals.

"Imagine where we are going today!" I said. You don't? Me either. We probably have the same amount of understanding of all this stuff going on around us, do we?"

I put my hand on the car, asking God to be our guide into the unknown!

I had a feeling deep inside we might have to move somewhere far away from our home and it was going to happen very soon.

"Let me check you out," I said. " I see.You're still wearing winter tires from 2007, right?Remember our last visit at the tire shop? We were advised to buy a new set of tires for you, because the ones you have on developed multiple microcracks, causing a hum on the highway". Some elements of the rubber were literally coming off! I gave a word to the repairman that this year would be the last year I use those. This time for sure. Guaranteed. I bought a set of summer tires. I planned to put them on in spring.

They're still sitting in my garage to this day.

It was still cold enough to put them on at negative 1°C at the end of February. But it was not the only problem with the car, as it turned out later.

The front ball joint on the driver's side needed replacement. It was a source of a hum in the car! Not the tires.

My cousin Vadim, along with his son Timofiy, eventually replaced one two years later, when we visited them in Germany. That part was in such a bad shape that it could easily seize up any moment on the highway, making a car flip over! I made another 3,000 kilometers on it before repair!

Someday, I will shake hands with my guardian angel and thank God for assigning such an attentive angel to me!

On the way to the tire shop, I decided to first fill up my car with fuel since I had less than half a tank.

Normally the gas station near us is almost unattended. Occasionally there might be a few cars in line, but very rare.

Today, there was a line several kilometers long! What's going on in this world? The drivers complained.

I had never seen drivers talking to each other much while standing in line. But not today. The drivers began to gather in groups along the road, getting out of their cars, energetically discussing the latest news. I started eavesdropping.

Did you hear that a war has just started? Where? In Ukraine? Unbelievable. What does it mean we got attacked? How did they dare? Swearing loudly, they weren't fully believing what they were saying.

Some planned to stay and not rush, thinking the news was still very fresh, some thought it still might be a sort of misunderstanding. News can deceive and exaggerate. Better to sleep on it.

Anyways, where should we go? Who is waiting for us anywhere?

I was standing there listening to their conversations, choosing not to share my raw plans with anyone. What did I know? I myself had multiple questions and zero answers.

"If only there was enough fuel here for all of us!" I thought to myself.

After a few hours of waiting, I finally reached the pump, filled up my car, and also filled a six-liter canister I found in the trunk. Sometimes it's good to have some junk in the trunk like this canister, I smiled to myself.

"From now on, we'll ration fuel to twenty liters per person," announced the gas station manager.

On the drive home, I thanked God for the fuel! Now we are good to go. Just quickly change the tires, pack a suitcase, and hit the road right away!

As we planned to stop by the supermarket on the way home, Tanya and I went together.

I love when she rides with me! We used to do everything together. Even when things don't go well sometimes, but since it's been done together, we never blame each other for the negative outcome. That's how it works in our family.

Tanya prefers safety more than anything else. I know that. It's out of the question. The family has to be protected and period. We had to buy enough food for the road.

As expected, half of the shelves in a crowded supermarket were empty. Still we got some food in the long run!

To our surprise, all five tire shops we checked on were closed! We saw a man, swearing loudly, angrily threw a stone into the yard of the tire shop owner. "The shop should be open 24/7!" He yelled.

"What tires are you talking about you need to replace?" Someone asked me at one of those tire shops. Don't you know that a war has started?"

4. A Long Journey

After praying boarding the car, we finally set off. We always pray for safe travels. Now we needed God's protection like never before!

About 10 p.m we left the house. It was dark and frosty. We joined the other travellers on a busy highway. Miscellaneous thoughts were constantly rushing through my head, one after another. I knew what it meant to be

- a father to my children
- a husband to my wife
- a brother to my four sisters
- a son to my parents
- an interpreter
- a builder
- a driver.

But I had no idea about what it meant to be a war refugee. I had seen on TV the consequences of armed conflicts, where people were forced to live in tents, being helped by organizations like the Red Cross.

Would such a fate await us? Where am I taking my family? What am I signing for?

Will we be safe?

We were comforted by the thought that soon we will come back home! It might take a week or two the longest. It's just a temporary misunderstanding. Nothing more, Calm down. I made several deep breaths but yet couldn't relax.

To almost every question from my wife and kids I replied that I do not know much what awaits down the road.

BUT

The Lord would definitely take care of us! He won't leave us nor forsake us. He promised that and I believe Him. Wasn't he faithful yesterday, today, and He will be forever the same? Anyplace we go! Our parents promised to pray for us, therefore we will be fine. God is good. And I know that He is. He goes ahead of us, protecting us with His angels. We are good, no worries. For now, we aren't hungry. We are clothed. Let's be satisfied with little for now!

Almost all the clothes I took were on me. Why would I need extra stuff if we are coming back in a short while? I didn't think much about what to take with me. Instead, I rather thought about how to fix the garage door, which suddenly stopped responding to the remote control in such an inappropriate moment. I thought about how to prepare the car for a long trip.

We wondered if we could find someone to temporarily live in our house to keep the lights on in our windows. Our house was robbed before and we wanted to do our best to prevent it in the future. Looting might happen at any moment, which, as it turned out later, did happen.

The individuals, guilty of this crime, were captured and tied to trees and electric poles with a scotch tape in public places. Anyone could photograph them and post their faces on social media.

We watered our plants, locked the doors, petted our animals, who we consider our family members, and left the keys with my parents. Later on, Tanya's aunt Galina, agreed to stay in our house for a while, to heat the wood stove, water the plants, and feed our pets. We were relieved at least in this realm!

The funds we had with us were divided into several parts and placed securely under our clothes. As logic dictated, it might happen so that someone of us would be for some reason apart from the group or might have no luggage with him. I hold all the passports inside of my travelling purse under my shirt to prevent displacement. We considered all possible scenarios.

Like Boy Scouts, we had better be prepared for any scenario! We relied on God and the instinct of survival in extreme situations.

Let these trials be the plot for the films and books!

It was already deep into the night.

I tried to keep the speed at 90-100 km/h, always in sixth gear, driving in economy mode as much as possible.

Gas stations on the highway were either closed, due to the absence of fuel, or had lengthy lines. Drivers had to spend long hours in those lines to get at least limited amount of fuel. We definitely didn't want to be one of them!

I couldn't even imagine how much fuel was wasted today by the drivers with Kyiv's license plates on! One driver told me that today he had to make a distance between Kyiv and Zhytomyr in six hours. Normally it takes just little bit longer than an hour!

Some drivers resorted to using bypass roads, while others navigated through fields, relying on local residents for directions to travel parallel to the highway toward Zhytomyr.

Big number of civilian cars on this stretch of highway were shot at by the occupiers!

Enemies broke into our land with a purpose to spread panic among civilians. They ambushed and fired at the cars of ordinary Ukrainians! The Kyiv-Zhytomyr highway later on was blocked on both sides by the Ukrainian military for two weeks.

For almost two weeks russian invaders disallowed Ukrainians to recover the bodies of killed drivers and passengers. Most of the time entire families were shot point-blank, some lying not far from their cars, trying to escape by running. It all resembled a scene from a horror movie.

Such images cut into your memory and remain there lifelong!

Anger and tears filled our eyes from the helplessness of being trapped in such circumstances which are far beyond your control! We felt so bad for those poor victims of circumstance! All of them were just Innocent civilians, who lived their lives and built plans for the future. No one of them have ever thought he would've died today!

Now, more than ever, it was time to be extra strong and resilient! Strong and resilient. We are the Ukrainians. Ukrainians never give up! Especially Daniela, who can't stand travelling long distances, asking us from time to time when we finally arrive. We will. Just wait some more. We will certainly arrive.

But deep in my head I myself would love to know the answer to that question. Arrive...where?

I was looking far into the highway laying down ahead of me. The same manner I tried to peek into the future, at least for a moment, wondering of what await us ahead.

We were driving without a navigator. But even if we had one, I wouldn't know what address to input.

For the first time in my life, I was simply driving right into the darkness, moving down the direction to nowhere...

5. Unexpected Road Hazards

The kids were peacefully resting in the back seat of the car, leaning on each other. They were warned out by asking questions they wanted to be answered.

The opposite lane of the highway was nearly empty, with only a few cars heading toward Kyiv. Occasionally, we passed concrete zigzag-shaped blocks and patrols of police officers along with Ukrainian military personnel, carefully inspecting the interiors of passing vehicles.

Gradually we started noticing the decreasing speed of cars in both lanes, and it became apparent that we were slowing down in speed.

We led conversations along the way just to keep our eyes open, recalling our trips to Crimea, to the Black Sea, to a place called Sunny Valley, where we used to camp by the sea.

On the way to Crimea, we often encountered similar traffic jams, especially on narrow stretches or in the mountains.

Our good friends and neighbors were following us in

their car, being afraid of getting lost. I kept them in my sight at all times. It was reassuring to know that we weren't alone. They didn't have a GPS either, and were worried to lose us from their sight.

Getting lost on the road to nowhere. How does that sound? But it is feels better to follow someone anyway.

All we had in our minds now was getting toward the Ukrainian-Polish border and finally crossing it, finding safety abroad.

I began to notice the traffic was slowing down even more, and soon we realised we could no longer keep moving efficiently. In low gears, I kept an eye on the fuel gauge, which showed I had about 60% of a tank left. I had never appreciated fuel as much as I did now!

It felt like a phone battery running out in the cold while we need it most, with no charger nearby!

The situation here was even worse. Even with money, we couldn't refuel the car, and no one would be willing to share even few liters of their fuel with you! Fuel is valued like gold in such circumstance!

I recalled one day during my shift in the supermarket I was witnessing customers emptying the shelves with the fuel cans, both expensive and cheap ones, disappearing one after another right before my eyes. People were probably sensing danger approaching. The shop assistants, like myself, were puzzled, watching them do it from afar.

The traffic had nearly come to a halt. We anxiously stared at the endless line of red taillights ahead.

Our Nissan Qashqai had never witnessed such abundance of fellow colleagues travelling along in the same time!

At that moment, we had no clue we were heading toward a forty-kilometer-long dead traffic jam.

By the next day, it would extend to **eighty** kilometers! Our friends got caught in it, an entire family with their small children in the car. They spent ENTIRE WEEK standing in it!

Drivers were trying to overtake each other, nervous and stressed out. Couple of times, we witnessed them confronting and pushing one another nearby their vehicles.

The road toward the border had the following construction. Two lanes going one way and two going the other, separated by a metal guardrail.

When we reached a gap in the guardrail and the turning point, a crazy idea crossed my mind. I rapidly threw it out my head. Bad thoughts visit my head from time to time. It happens. Just neglect them and keep on moving.

I was even afraid to voice it. I know exactly what my sweetheart thinks about safety and she is absolutely right! The entire family is here now! All precious people are gathered inside of the small populous space!

With a faint voice, I suggested "What if we try moving against the flow of traffic with hazard lights on? We are running out of precious fuel and can't stay where we are now."

Since the outside temperature was -1°C, drivers in the traffic jam kept their engines running to heat their car interiors. Most of the time the entire families were aboard in those vehicles.

Some families later on that coming week were leaving their vehicles making bonfires out of their own belongings to get warm!

I didn't have much time to think and had to make a decision. I had no clue how far ahead down the road would be another gap in the guardrail. With the words "God help me" I decided to take the risk.

Leaving our lane at the turning point, we slowly began moving against the flow of traffic.

Our friends didn't hesitate and followed our lead.

Our lives were now hanging by a thread, and all we cared about now was purely the chance to survive!

We have a saying in Ukraine.

"Either you're the master, or you're done!" It has a rhyme in our language.

I was now risking not only my family lives but also our friends' family following behind!

It seems like it is better sometimes not to hear what others might be saying about you behind your back! Those "others" could easily be aboard the other car. Maybe my friends weren't my friends anymore?

Not fully realizing what I was doing, I calculated the risks.

We were moving again in economical mode. Except... against the flow of traffic!

Like never before, in the middle of a pitch-black night, had I felt so sober and alert!

I felt like I grew wings behind my back! Without Redbull.

I bet even my trusty Qashqai, if one could speak, would have said something not very nice. Friend, It's good sometimes you can't talk!

There wasn't even a hint of sleepiness with everybody now! I definitely didn't need any coffee on the moment!

It felt like this was all happening in a dream, or rather a nightmare. Like you eat some heavy stuff and went to bed. But unfortunately it wasn't.

Welcome to the harsh reality!

Looking in the rearview mirror, I noticed besides our friends' car, several other vehicles had joined our convoy. Over time, their numbers grew. None of them seemed to want to pass me for some reason! Maybe they liked my economy driving mode? On the highway in the right lanes they didn't!

I felt like a frontier goose flying in a V-shaped formation for a good while, with no one willing to replace me!

The ongoing vehicles acted out weird as well.

Some applied their bright high beams, flashing directly into my eyes. Man it burns like a fire!

Some turned their high beams on and kept moving in my direction the whole time, swerving not far from my hood the last second. That's refreshing.

Honking their horns I was reminded that I was in the wrong lane. Seriously?

It wasn't a sort of "chicken game". Or "Need for Speed. Hot Pursuit"

My eyes permanently were searching for the U-turn gap to fall into, hoping to finally get back into my lane. I saw a spot where I could dive in. But soon I realized I couldn't take it!

The sharp U-turn ahead would send us right back against the flow of traffic afterward!

I didn't know that. You see, I had zero practice driving on the opposite side of the road! I didn't consider that when I made the decision to end up where I was now.

Not losing hope, I wanted to see what caused the traffic jam ahead. Perhaps, by some miracle, we'd return to our lane somehow? But I was unable to fix the situation.

I silently prayed, gripping the steering wheel tightly. What a strange night it had been! My wife wanted to hint at something during the mad race, but I asked her not to speak to me on the moment. For some reason I didn't feel like speaking. I needed 110% concentration to deal with the mess I have just created.

Our kids were very much awake in the backseat, being fully aware of the danger their dad brought them into! Daniel was recording some episodes on his phone.

Kids trusted their daddy completely even in those circumstance! Maybe pretended. He was doing his best right now teaching them a safety lesson! Everyone could witness how does the theory diverged from practice. It was all happening right before their eyes!

I recalled a dreadful accident happened with a young couple in their twenties from our church. They underwent a head-on collision with a drunk driver moving towards them in their lane making 100 miles an hour!

From the head-on collision the husband and wife died on a spot, but their baby daughter survived, sitting in her child seat behind the front seat. And now, here I am, the number one lawbreaker in the world! Ahead of a group of drivers following my example!

I tried not to look at my wife's frightened eyes, who was feeling exactly like a kamikaze prisoner.

I remembered once, when she had been with me during winter and I hadn't yet changed to winter tires. A very bad idea.

We sled sideways across the highway for about a hundred meters!

A car coming toward us seemed to pass right through us! I only remember shouting "Jesus!"

We remained on the road without a single scratch! Later, Tanya told me she had a thought to jump out of the car onto the road during the skid!

Now, we needed nothing less than a miracle. Jesus, help us one more time I beg!

Gradually, I noticed in the distance the red taillights of other desperate individuals on the same lane. I felt sudden relief. Finally I was following someone!

My eyes burned like a fire from the high beams. It felt itching like after welding without protective goggles! It turned out I wasn't the only one who had lost his mind here! I met my fellow colleagues on the road! As though we had just broken through the cage gates, rushing toward freedom!

The movement slowed down and finally stopped here too.

Military personnel, together with the police, began directing traffic back into the proper lane. With their help, we finally ended up in the right place.

I noticed my hands were shaking like the autumn leaves in the wind and I spoke with difficulty. I was trembling all over, even though it was warm inside of the car. It was somewhat hard to form coherent sentences.

Over time, I realized more gray hairs had appeared at my temples.

I wonder, why has that happened?

6. Crossing the Border

We spent the entire next day waiting in an endless line at the border.

It wasn't until the evening of the following day that we finally reached it.

Our friends decided to return home, as they were exhausted from the journey with their daughter, who has a severe form of Down syndrome and heart failure. She wasn't accustomed to long and exhausting trips.

We hugged them one last time, praying for God's protection over both our families.

Upon approaching the border and passport control area we learned that Ukraine's parliament, the Verkhovna Rada, which had been in session all night, passed a law prohibiting men aged 18 to 65 cross the border with foreign countries.

While we were leaving home, we knew all family members were allowed to travel together.

Hearing this news, my wife and kids started crying, trying to hide their tears. Besides some sobbing there was silence in the car. I didn't know what to say either. I just shrugged my shoulders. It felt like a lump had stuck in my throat. We truly didn't know what to do now.

Was everything we just did in vain? Really? Just like that? Besides we owned only one car.

Taking a huge risk for themselves, my wife and kids decided to leave the car with me!

I will never forget the level of sacrifice of my wife and children made that day! It's like giving up your spot in a rescue boat to someone else, jeopardizing your own life. They had no idea what lay ahead for them, now stranded without a car!

That's the level of self-sacrifice in my family I am proud of!

There was no other transportation available at the border to head back into Ukraine.

Suddenly, we noticed multiple people from all over leaving their vehicles streaming toward a bus that had just stopped. There were no markings on it. More likely it was an ordinary international bus with Ukrainian license plates. For some reason one was lacking passengers at that moment.

A temporary shelter solution?

We saw a group of people on the roadside being ordered to lie down on the asphalt with their hands covering their heads during air raid sirens. Their clothes turned dirty and wet.

In such a state, they would be starting their new lives somewhere in Europe!

Not knowing anything else about the bus but seeing so many people streaming down to board it, we decided to join them too. It seemed like they knew something. Hastily, we began dividing food, money, and gathering belongings.

I'm still very sad about the fact that in the chaos I lost my wedding ring and couldn't find it! I had it in my finger for twenty years of our marriage! Our world was falling apart in pieces.

Since we hadn't planned this journey with suitcases, nothing was organized the way it should have been otherwise. One thing we figured out for sure. We couldn't miss that bus! We had no plan B.

Our daughter Daniela cried inconsolably while sitting in the front row of seats on the bus. She was told to stay in her seat no matter what and wait while our luggage was loaded into the storage compartment, as directed by the driver.

From that moment until now, she has been terrified of being left alone. Even nowadays, in public places, holding tightly to my hand, she constantly asks me not to leave her even for a moment!

Through her tears, she removed her necklace and handed it to me, saying, "If we never see each other again, let this be a memory of me for you!"

Imaging to hear something like that from your child? It feels nothing else but a knife stabbing right into your heart!

She took off her neck her necklace and handed one to me weeping aloud! Earlier she did something similar to her grandmother, saying goodbye to her.

I had never seen in my life so many men in tears on their faces hugging and kissing their families! They were parting from their loved ones now. Many of them forever.

Nearly all the women and children, some of them infants, were transferred from cars to the bus. Waving goodbye to their husbands and daddies standing outside, blowing them kisses, they wrote messages and drew hearts on the windows of the bus. I stood outside the bus with those men. I wished the bus would delay its departure just a little longer! I wanted to prolong the moment because I didn't know when or if we would meet again.

My sons' eyes were wide open, filled with despair. They didn't even know of what to say. For the first time in their lives, they found themselves in such a situation. They silently watched the events unfolding around them.

It felt as if you were dead, yet still alive!

We will never be able to forget what we have experienced that day! We were consumed by an overwhelming sense of helplessness and despair. You witnessed the moment your family ceases to be whole anymore.

I wish all the enemies of Ukraine to feel exactly same thing what we felt.

7. Wonderful News

While on the bus, Tetiana received a text message on her phone.

She had been conserving her battery, which was down to just a few percent. Still decided to open it, Tanya found a message from Anna, the widow of a deacon from our church, a man of extraordinary kindness and integrity, one of the best people I've ever met in my life.

He had passed away just a year ago at a tragically young age. He struggled with sugar diabetes. Doctors said that stress and anxiety added up and eventually shortened his life.

He left behind a deep scar in the hearts of his wife and their young son, Bohdan, who almost same age as Daniel. We had a tradition with that family. Every New Year's Eve we would gather together and pray at midnight for our families, our country, and our ministry. We deeply miss you our dear brother!

Anna educated Tanya on a new amendment to the law that allowed certain groups of individuals to cross the border, namely Individuals with disabilities Men before 18 and older then 65 Large families with three children or more, under age 18.

David, at that time, was 17 and a half years old. "We qualify!" Tanya joyfully exclaimed to the children!

The passports for all four of them had already been collected by a border official. She took them and left the bus.

Tanya ran after her, pleading to return her passports. The official informed her that in case they leave the bus, they would be stranded on the street without transportation.

Tanya and kids spent five hours inside the bus waiting in line.

The border line was right in the middle of the fields, far away from any obvious infrastructure.

On her way back to the bus, she asked another border officer if he knew anything about the new law. He replied that they were aware of it but it is not his responsibility to inform travelers about one. "People are responsible for knowing this themselves," he said.

She explained desperately, "We have three kids here, all under eighteen! My husband left us here, but he's here, in its vicinities, just few kilometers away!"

The official reiterated that if she leaves the bus now, she and her children would be left all by themselves on the street alone with their luggage.

Despite this, Tanya was determined. She retrieved her bags from the luggage compartment and left the bus.

Left standing in the cold, they prayed for a miracle!

Only God knew how badly we wanted to be together as a family again! And now, finally, we had a chance. A small one, but still a chance!

Meanwhile, I had driven few kilometers back toward Ukraine and stopped at a gas station. Now I had to drive through the night without my sweetheart's massages on my ears she always does to keep me awake on long drives!

I thought about napping for a couple of hours before going back home. The car was cold and empty. I couldn't relax and warm up. Realizing I wouldn't be able to sleep anyway, I decided to wait inside the warm gas station and recharge my phone.

My heart was heavy over everything that had happened lately. I was like beaten up. The only thing I really wanted is to be with my my family again. Even from a distance! The state of fatigue was secondary, though I still had to make another six hundred kilometers towards my empty home.

My life was about to change BIG time.

It's quite interesting that at home, it wasn't just us who were happy to be all together. All three of our dogs were not less excited to see us back everytime, greeting us at the door!

Am I now going to grill barbecue just for myself? Mow the lawn and maintain the pool water just for my own purposes? Eat all the fruits from our trees by my own? Watch movies and cartoons being all alone? Walk our shepherd Elsa by the river first time by myself?

Daniela once made a great association regarding our family. She said that we all represent a hand. Five fingers are five of us! A hand can't fully function without even one of its fingers missing. We are always one and inseparable!

When Tanya called to share the news with me, my joy was just overflowing! I praised God for another miracle He made for us right now! I know He is close to brokenhearted. Everyone at the gas station could tell something is happening with that strange guy over there! They would have more things to watch If I had Daniela here with me! We have a tradition. When we are super happy, we would jump for joy, holding one another by the hands. When we're happy, everyone knows we're happy!

I told Tanya I'm right on my way now and I would meet her soon. I would never ever miss a chance to be reunited with my family! I missed them already.

Taking my seat at the wheel I looked around. I saw a massive line of cars stretching for kilometers! The line extended far beyond the gas station, with no visible end. Besides there was no visible movement forward at all.

I knew that line better than anyone else in here, spending there the entire day prior to this moment. Once I already reached the passport control area. It would be just another miracle to make it there any time soon!

Watching the line from afar, thinking of the impossible, I recalled something funny.

One day we watched a cartoon named Spirit. My favorite scene was there when the horse's owner, a man from an ancient Indian tribe in America, came up and retrieved his horse back. Now he is sitting on his horseback at the edge of a canyon, right in front of bottomless abyss. Chased by armed soldiers, the man was saying to himself, judging the horse's intention:

"Oh no!"

Spirit, preparing for a jump, in his mind was saying:

"Oh yes!"

Drawing on my recent experience, I was setting my mind to drive in the oncoming lane this time toward the international border.

Calculating the risks I couldn't fully comprehend what I was getting myself into. Not even in my wildest dreams. I prayed a prayer for God's protection on me and slowly began moving.

It was nighttime. Visibility was poor. I would never dare do anything like that at an international border in-between two countries, in front of so many witnesses!

I started moving forward gradually gaining speed. Now I'm shifting the fourth gear, staying extremely alert and attentive. My headlights were piercing the darkness in front of me.

Exactly like in a song of Beatles

Suddenly

From the middle of nowhere a figure grew up right in front of my hood!

I applied extreme braking. I saw a silhouette of an individual dressed in military uniform, blocking the road with a machine gun in his hands, aimed both at me and my car.

Was that a movie filming episode or something? Don't scare me like that!

Still with my doors and windows closed l could hear the male voice shouting

"Get out of the car now with your hands up!"

Seeing his serious expression, I realized that the man in a camouflage uniform wasn't joking with me at all! The only thing I was happy now that my family hadn't witnessed that part!

Moments later, I stood before him, my hands raised, staring down the barrel of his gun.

"What do you think you're doing right now?" he yelled.

There was a long pause on my end. I kind of swallowed my tongue.

"You think you're smarter here than everyone else? I have the right to shoot you and your car right now!

Another pause. He continued:

Do you realize you're setting a bad example for everyone standing there in line? What would I be supposed to do in case everybody else would follow your lead?"

There was even longer pause.

Knowing my Quasqai can't speak, I knew it's my turn to say something wise.

The border official didn't know that when I'm scared I have hard time speaking! I know that. I'd already tried it earlier today. It works every time!

My voice trembling, I started explaining to the border guard about the newly passed law that allowed large families with three or more children under age 18 to cross the border.

Hearing this, he lowered his voice slightly still keeping me in his sights under the gun.

It seemingly was a good start. At least he was listening. And I was able to speak!

I explained that right this moment my wife and children are standing on the border crossing line, waiting for me at passport control. We had already spent entire day standing here in line, from very start to finish!

"We'll see about that," he said, pulling out his phone to call his superior.

While he explained the situation, I stood with my hands still raised, catching the curious stares of drivers in the long line. For them, this must have been an unexpected free show, something to break the monotony of the wait! I was standing right in their spotlight! Interesting enough. What's gonna happen with that guy right there now?

To be or not to be?

"Yes, there is such a law," he finally said.

"But just so you know, if I had shot you before finding out, I still would have been within my rights!" With that, he finally lowered his weapon and disappeared back into the darkness.

What a day had it been today!

I don't remember praying so fervently in my life, thanking God aloud for delivering and preserving me once again!

God has given me many extra birthdays that day!

8. Where to Next?

We were handed a small slip of paper with a handwritten number "5," a stamp and a signature.

While waiting there, I suggested to clean out the car a bit prior to entering Polish vicinities. Another check-up is waiting right ahead. The car should be clean.

Soon I realised I can't find that official manuscript with number five on it. I must have thrown it away by accident during that process!

After tearing through the entire car looking for one, I went to the same trash bin I used not long ago, and started searching for my bag with a light in my hand.

Good thing that the garbage bin contained only my bag solely sitting inside! At that moment, I felt like I had nothing else left to lose today. Not even my dignity now!

What kind of night is this I wonder?

Everything feels kind of surreal, like in a wild dream! I started to wonder if my mind was cracking under the stress.

I came to the moment I felt like laughing! Maybe it was

some kind of coping mechanism? I'd experienced it before in moments of extreme tension.

The Polish border guard—his back emblazoned with the words Straż Graniczna (Border Guard) approached our vehicle asking for documents. I proudly put on top of a stack of passports the slip of paper with the number 5.

"Five!" It sounded to me like a high five!

Where was my pat on the back for everything I'd just gone through you keep that slip in your hand? He had no idea where it had been just a moment ago!

But instead of a sort of compliment, I was told about something else was still missing, an international Green Card insurance document. My Ukrainian insurance wasn't valid here, and without one I couldn't legally drive on Polish roads!

Perhaps, judging by my recent driving skills, I would probably needed double insurance?I got it now! What else could go wrong today? Or tonight? Or today and tonight combined?

I was smiling to myself wagging my head while standing in line at the border insurance bureau. I was the only happy person standing in a line in here! The other people were watching furtively at me. I didn't care.

At dawn I managed to purchase the new insurance! I had here my first-ever conversation in Polish. I spoke to them in Ukrainian and they answered me back in Polish. That how it works. It's just incredible how people can understand one another!

I noticed the name of the insurance bureau was called "Odesa," even though it was Polish firm. How ironic was that! We were placed nowhere in the world now near Ukrainian city Odesa!

Finally, we completed the long-awaited process of crossing the border. What a relief. Thank you God! Many times thank you!

It was the longest crossing we ever had so far. Finally we did it! Congratulations! Up to that point, our only thought, our singular goal had been is to reach safety.

Standing in line everyone of us was thinking the same thought. Where are we going now?

In our imagination, we invisioned vehicles with Polish license plates, speeding confidently down the highway. They were heading toward homes or destinations where they were waited for. Their navigation screens likely glowed brightly, guiding them forward. Or perhaps they simply knew the route by heart!

Here someone is being welcomed at the border with flowers, hugs, and warm reunions! How sweet is that!

Resembling caged animals, suddenly released from a zoo into the wild, we were about to enter a foreign country!

It was like one of those movie scenes, where a hungry person stares into a restaurant window, watching diners enjoy warm meals at candlelight.

I remembered meeting numerous people at Boryspil International Airport over the years, holding signs with their names on, doing my best to stand out. The moment someone saw their name on a sign, their eyes lit up!

Soon after we met, they were not alone anymore in a new place! Someone is expecting them here with a big welcoming smile on his face!

No matter what may happen, God is always in control,

isn't He? Always! He is a Way Maker! I was doing my best to comfort my family.

Before the war began, my son David had met a girl named Anyuta. They met at a youth meeting event at the church and exchanged their phone numbers. All her family lived near us in a newly built neighborhood, though we'd never met before.

A few months earlier, they'd bought an apartment in Kraków so their daughter could study in Poland. They had Polish heritage and a residence permit.

While standing in the long line on the other side of a border, David texted her, hoping for a reply. She was the only connection we had! Our only hope!

When her response came, tears of joy filled our eyes.

"Don't go anywhere, her dad Olexander has told us. Meet you at the border. We're about 300 kilometers away. Please don't worry. We will be there for you!"

What a joy and relief did we feel that moment! Thank you Jesus for the people like that! People we barely knew, were willing to drive 300 kilometers, in the middle of the night to meet us!

It was a direct answer from God, nothing else!

Despite being exhausted, Olexander drove long distance to reach us. We thanked God for the glimmer of light pierced through the darkness! We felt incredible!

All we wanted now was a warm place with a bed to rest in.

How long were we spending standing in a border line? Five long hours Tanya spent with the kids on a bus, while Olexander was driving here to meet us! Additionally he waited about same amount of hours in his car, standing on the border!

Next moment we were giving and receiving big hugs, appreciating his care and gracious gesture.

We followed Olexander, with Ukrainian license plates on his car, being simply overwhelmed with emotions! Tears streaming down our cheeks, we thanked him for his kindness and willingness to help!

Following after his car through Poland, we noticed Roman-alphabet road signs. They looked different. We immensely enjoyed seeing a car with Ukrainian license plate right before our eyes!

It's interesting enough how your perspectives shift. You begin to reevaluate your entire life.

Like electricity, which you took for granted, until it's gone. Many things you had before felt so precious now!

We started to cherish Ukrainian people we were meeting on our way, our language, our traditions, even Ukrainian food brands! Finishing our food supplies with Ukrainian brand names on it we were doing our best to prolong the pleasure! It felt like we had been severed from our homeland. Like an umbilical cord had just been cut.

Welcome to a new world!

At a gas station, I refilled the tank and felt an unexpected sense satisfaction. Something I'd hardly appreciated so much before. It was like a drink of water in a hot day! Qashqai loved it. For so long I used to fix my eyes on the fuel gauge, praying it would freeze and not move!

Olexander, driving his fast Lexus, wanted us to go faster. I had to explain to him that I would love to, but I had overloaded vehicle and, of course, I had my ancient tires! Besides, I got used to driving economically, treating fuel like gold.

Remember how Jacob from the Bible once told Esau, his brother, after encountering with him, who was with his men on horseback, not to wait for him as he was moving slowly with his family and herds. Now it was me!

The strong coffee from the gas station couldn't keep my eyes open anymore. I am blessed for Tanya who had her driver's license with her. She is an experienced and a safe driver. She wouldn't have to deal now with much mess, since she had the guy here who did all the dirty job for all of us!

Exhausted, later we decided to stop and sleep on the roadside with the hazard lights on.

As I drifted off, I saw images of the endless line of cars, a talking Qashqai, border guards with their weapons, and all the unanswered questions lingered in my mind...

9. Trying to Find Our Bearings

What warm acceptance we received from Oleksandra's wife Olga and her daughter Anyuta! What a sweet family! Such warm embraces proceeded from the people we were meeting for the first time. It was simply astonishing!

They told us to eat and rest first. Only then we will talk. We felt so good. Finally, we were safe and comfy. Now we could relax and take a hot bath, in which I almost drifted away!

At that point, we had been traveling for 52 hours straight.

We slept through the entire next day and night. After resting, I had a headache and felt like going back to bed again."You can't sleep this long!" our friends suggested. "Let's go for a walk! We'll show you something really incredible nearby."

We didn't realize that were were only a few minutes' walk away from the Schindler's Factory, made famous by the movie "Schindler's List", one of my favorites. A story about saving people's lives during the war. It's simply incredible! Incredible emotions.

Since it was Sunday, we couldn't walk inside the factory. However, outside was a large photo gallery of former factory workers. These people hadn't come here out of choice or their desire. They were inside those walls because their lives were in danger and they needed a rescue shelter.

Think of that. Who would have thought history could repeat itself in 2022! Right in the middle of Europe. Again?

Soon, nine million Ukrainian citizens would be seeking refuge and safety around the world.

We learned shortly that every media outlet here was broadcasting live updates about the events in Ukraine. Poland was overwhelmed by the massive influx of Ukrainian refugees and was asking people to move further into the EU, if possible.

Yet, the Polish people treated us with incredible kindness and reception. They were curious to hear our firsthand accounts of what was happening. Ordinary citizens opened their homes, with tens, even hundreds of thousands of its citizens, willing to host us. Their generosity left an unforgettable impression!

Later, across train and bus stations in host countries, volunteers and charities would help refugees navigate, offering temporary shelter and assistance with paperwork.

We were in turmoil. Where should we go next?

Tanya's mother and stepfather live in Italy, but we consciously avoided going there, not wanting to burden them with our unknown visit duration. Several countries were ready to take Ukrainians in, but we had little to no information on where we might find support.

Unsure of where to go, we set up to move further into the EU, freeing up space in Poland for other refugees. At least we had our own car, which allowed us to keep moving!

Since it was Sunday, we couldn't get and replace tires for the car. In Poland, everything is closed on Sundays except emergency services. Shops, restaurants, and auto repair shops are all shut down, as running businesses on Sundays is frowned upon. Many people attend church, and their faith is reflected in the way they care for their neighbours!

Three years later, Poland is still hosting over a million Ukrainians

As I scrolled through my phone contacts, I tried to reach out to people I knew—starting with those who had visited Ukraine multiple times.

What I discovered next I thought I had many friends. But suddenly my eyes were opened up. I realized that people I called friends were mere my acquaintances. Many of those acted as though this tragedy didn't concern them personally at all. They did their best trying to explain me why exactly they couldn't help.

There is a true saying, "A friend in need is a friend indeed," couldn't have been more accurate. Real friendship is something else entirely.

Finally, I came across Kees, a Dutchman, married to a Ukrainian lady. They've been always kind and friendly with people. Their family lived near Zhytomyr, where Kees worked in horticulture, skilfully managing several hectares of land.

Anticipating the war, Kees had moved his family to the Netherlands. Unlike us, he had been following international news, which made the likelihood of an invasion clear to him. I personally didn't share his perspective at the time, believing to the last minute that disputes would be resolved diplomatically.

Kees turned out to be a true friend and a noble person in the full sense of the word. His assistance will be remembered for a lifetime!

After the conversation, he assured us that we should come to his country with zero hesitation! By the time we arrive there would be a place for us to stay and a job waiting! He restored our faith in humanity, being the only person offering clarity in those uncertain moments! We prayed, entrusted ourselves to God's will. We felt peace and decided to head toward the Netherlands next day.

By that time we had no idea where the Netherlands was placed on the map! But we liked its name! It sounded somewhat romantic and magical to us. The Netherlands. The name sounds plural. A large family, also in plural, would be about to be right on its way there!

Soon, the Netherlands would become home to 100,000 Ukrainian refugees.

On Monday morning, we decided to commence our journey.

We remembered we had Ukrainian currency with us, equivalent to about $3,000. We had better exchange it here, we thought, since Poland borders with Ukraine. Who would want our Ukrainian money in the Netherlands, far away from here? It was enough to keep us afloat for a while. We relied on that budget as on a safety net, ensuring we wouldn't end up on the street.

However, at the currency exchange place has prepared a "surprise" for us. Soon we hit a harsh reality.

After calling his boss, the bank worker announced that devaluation of our national currency was extreme. Nobody gives prognosis what awaits our economy. Therefore, the maximum they could offer us for our savings was EUR 300!

EUR 300?! That amount of money would be exactly enough to cover just few tanks of fuel for our car! We found ourselves standing between two countries with barely enough resources to survive.

Being in extreme state of mind I recalled another good acquaintance of mine. How could I forget him? He called me his friend! A well-off man I had interpreted for over 15 years. He visited Ukraine almost every year. Every time he was telling me he considered my family as his own. That's nice to hear! He even invited us to visit his country one day! Desperate, at my wits end, I contacted him, asking for assistance. He asked for my bank card details. He sounded understanding and compassionate.

He stopped answering my calls ever since.

Wow, it hurts! He taught me a valuable lesson not to expect anything from anybody. It was a painful lesson though. He was absolutely right! No one owes you anything indeed! Everyone has their own life, it's joys and struggles.

At the same time we were meeting people with big hearts on our way from whom we expected nothing, but who ended up helping us the most! Such moments are remembered forever.

We were learning to put our trust in God and Him only. He is the One who never let you down.

Even as the ground beneath seem to crumble.

10. An Angel?

A few hours later, we were standing on the highway in the direction toward the Netherlands.

Since roaming charges had drained our phone accounts, we no longer had internet access. All we had was an address in the Netherlands and about 15-20 screenshots of maps with key turns and junctions along the route.

The journey would take us through Poland, Germany, and into the Netherlands a total of 1,200 kilometers.

Oleksandr gave us a final hug, turning away so we wouldn't see the tears in his eyes! He understood that it would be a challenge for us. We had next to no money, no internet, and no certainty. But we had God in our hearts and our hearts were full of hope that He will guide us! He never let us down, why He should do now? We trust Him now and always will! He was our source of bravery. Believe in Him and don't be afraid.

Before we set out we stopped to fill the gas tank and

check the fluids. I always do it before long travels. Quasqai knows.

Opening the hood, I wondered how well we'd manage on the unfamiliar roads ahead? How would we supposed to navigate using just a bunch static maps?

It made me marvel at how resourceful people used to be back in the day, relying on paper maps folded ten times sitting in their glove compartments!

And here we are, without anyone to ask for directions, especially taking bypass roads. We didn't know the language, and with night approaching we might end up navigating by the stars! Just follow the North Star! For that you've got to be a real goose! The last thing I needed now is to take a wrong turn, waste fuel, get extra portion of stress and lose precious time.

Suddenly I felt an urge to look back at the car with a trailer that had just pulled up at the gas pump. It wasn't just a simple urge. I absolutely had to do it now!

So I did. Well, it looks like I'm looking at an average car standing right in front of me. Nothing special. The highway is nearby after all with multiple vehicles all over around here.

But the next moment I saw something made my jaw drop in astonishment. I called my wife and asked her if she sees the same thing I do. Just like myself she wasn't sure what exactly she was supposed to look at.

Then I pointed to the Dutch license plate on the car standing in front of us!

A driver, staring at the gas pump screen, was peacefully fueling his car, clearly preparing for a long trip. Better we were very much hoping that his trip would be long!

He definitely had no clue yet he was the answer to our

prayers! There he stood, calmly refueling his car, completely unaware of the intense gaze directed his way.

Within moments, I was standing in front of him, introducing myself with a smile on my face. I wondered, if by any chance he was heading towards the Netherlands? I desperately wanted to hear him say yes.

A lengthy pause here. Does he speak any English? Sorry I don't speak neither Polish nor Dutch. I didn't hear a single word from him yet.

He gave me a suspicious look, from head to toe. His face was just one huge question mark.

Why would that guy be curious about where I was going? What could he possibly want from me?

I realized he probably didn't have enough practice talking to strangers at gas stations. Did I? As if I did that sort of talk every day!

Nothing special. I'm just curious to find out how people react on all kinds of silly stuff! Hello! Wave your hand. You're on a hidden camera!

I swallow my pride and was asking for a favor. I was glancing back and forth between him and the NL license plate, adorned with a ring of stars.

Yellow license plates with blue stars! Beautiful. Astonishing. Colors of Ukraine. I am watching at almost Ukrainian license plates!

Seeing me strangely gazing at his license plate, he curiously glanced at ours. His expression changed. He told me just to wait while he paid for the gas and suggested we meet in the parking lot.

"Yes! I was saying to myself on the way back to my car.

It's already something! It's just simply incredible! Thank You Jesus for Your miracles!"

Soon, we were all together inspecting my car adding up some engine oil.

We felt like we were speaking to an angel who goes under name Matheus! He treated us with such kindness as we were his own children. God Himself had sent him to meet us here at this very moment of our journey!

Do you know that the Bible says angels can take on human form and speak to people? Who would've thought we'd meet someone 1,200 kilometers away from his home, on the other side of Europe, whom we'd end up trailing behind all the way to the Netherlands!

Mattheus was towing a trailer with a sticker indicating a speed limit of 90 km/h in a red circle. That was our ideal, fuel efficient cruising speed! Even in this, our loving Heavenly Father had taken care of us!

When we stopped for lunch, our mysterious stranger shared his sandwiches with us, being curious who we are visiting in the Netherlands. He lived 100 kilometers away from our destination.

He showed us photos of his family and his daughter on his phone, who lived in a town called Woudenberg, a name that meant nothing to us at that time.

But. A few months later, Tanya would be offered a teaching job- not just anywhere in the Netherlands, but exactly in the beautiful town of Woudenberg! More than that. For a while, my wife would stay with the family of his daughter, whose photo we were now looking at displayed on his phone!

For the next night and day in a row we followed our

mysterious angel heading toward the North Sea towards the Dutch coast.

Whenever he stopped we stopped. Whenever he ate we ate. Whenever he slept we slept. By dawn of the next we began to notice increasing intensity of yellow Dutch license plates showing up on the highway.

We stopped at the first gas station in the Netherlands ,where we learned, that since now on our paths would diverge. His road veered right, while ours went left.

"You have the address, right?" he asked. We tried contacting Kees with our phone, connecting to filling station's WI-FI, but our phone still wasn't working right.

Sensing our uncertainty, he called Kees from his phone, letting him know we made it this far. He removed the GPS navigator from his dashboard, entered our destination, and handed it to us. He fixed it at the windshield of our vehicle with the words "You need this more than I do now" he went his way.

We promised to mail it back to him. But we didn't. Later on, Tanya would personally handed one to his daughter in Woudenberg!

Sometimes angels really do walk among us!

11. New Realities

The GPS led us to a cozy house near a canal.

Like lifeblood coursing through veins, the canals nourish the Dutch lands with water.

Windmills lift it from one level to another. There are hundreds of them here! Some are over 300 years old and hold historical significance.

On the way, we passed colorful houses, each unique in shape and design. It felt as though we'd entered a fairytale world inhabited by gnomes and fairies!

Cyclists zipped along the red paths in all directions, their faces smiling despite the rain and wind. There are more bicycles in this country than people!

Life must be good for these people here, we thought, while back home, our people were being bombed and killed!

The door of the house opened, and we met Kees's good friends. Their pleasant, smiling Dutch faces warmly welcomed us into their charming home!

The decor was tasteful, reflecting the local culture. In the center of the living room were sturdy antique leather sofas and chairs. Fresh flowers, drinks, and cookies adorned the table. After enjoying hot tea with Dutch cookies, we felt ourselves drifting toward sleep. The calm and coziness were irresistible!

However, as we soon learned, we wouldn't be staying here. Instead, we were headed to another home—the residence of Jan, Kees's former business partner. The two of them had once run a landscaping business growing ornamental bushes and shrubs near Jan's house.

Here, nearly every home is accompanied by fields stretching across several hectares, complete with tractors and equipment.

Workers, always punctual, arrive daily early in the morning. Being even a minute or two late is considered unacceptable! Lunch breaks start precisely on time, and no one lingers a moment longer than scheduled.

I was told a story about a local boy and girl who were dating but broke up because one day she was late to a date! The boy left the meeting spot, concluding that punctuality was a non-negotiable quality for a future spouse!

I'm sure it was a make up story they pass from generation to generation.

Jan's home was surrounded by fields where wild hares roamed freely. From the window, we watched ducks, swans, and other birds going about their lives, seemingly oblivious to our presence. Killing a swan here incurs a fine of a couple thousand euros!

Near the house lived two decorative pigs that snorted

loudly. Here, pets can be anything—a goat, a horse, a sheep, a hare, and even chickens and roosters!

These animals are meant to teach children responsibility from a young age. How beautiful and thoughtful is that! We love all kinds of animals a lot!

By the way, kids can officially start working here at age thirteen!

Our daughter, Daniela, immediately bonded with a friendly cat and dog. She told our hosts about the five cats and three dogs we have back home. We had pictures of them in our phones to show the hosts what our life in Ukraine used to look like.

Windows in smaller towns and villages are never covered in the evenings. Everything around is visible. Due to the lack of sunlight, the windows are as large as possible, sometimes resembling an aquarium!

There was a law back in the day that prohibited covering windows, so people got used to it and still do so these days. The police needed to see what was happening inside, having unobstructed access to houses and properties. Because of this, there are no fences here, except for hedges. Anyone who installs one might arouse suspicion.

Peeping through someone's window at night, you suddenly notice that folks inside are watching you too! You can even wave to them, and they will wave back!

Soon, we were flipping through their family album and meeting members of their large extended family.

They settled us on the second floor, which offered a lovely view of the fields and their bustling farm.

Before long, we joined in, learning new skills in managing the plants alongside their workers.

The land here constantly requires fresh topsoil to counteract water saturation. Dig down just 20 centimeters, and you'll hit water. To build foundations, they drive 18-meter concrete piles into the ground!

In Amsterdam, where this wasn't always possible, many houses now lean, supporting each other like a united monolith.

Watching David and Daniel at work was a joy. They quickly mastered tractors and forklifts and drove those with pleasure. They learned so fast!

At just 14, Daniel could stack crates four levels high in the warehouse! He often received compliments and even had his photo taken quite a few times. The boys enjoyed their time behind the wheel, and the locals were eager to teach them the ropes.

Not long after, a new family offered us a separate home on their milk farm.

We now had our own space, complete with a key to the front door! Their milk farm, about three kilometers aside from the landscaping business, housed 300 cows and vast fields.

It amazed us that so few people managed such a large operation. Machines fed, cleaned, and milked the cows, working day and night with music playing in the background! Milk trucks arrived like self-service stations, filling their tanks with what was perhaps the best milk we'd ever tasted!

At the entrance to the farm stood a giant statue of a red cow—a national symbol of pride, often seen even at airports. After tasting the fresh milk, we understood the big reason why. It was far superior to what's been sold in supermarkets!

Corola and Arnold van Dorp, our new home owners, graciously provided to us a six-liter plastic bucket to fill with milk directly from the tank's spigot! The locals here would hardly lock any doors. All the gates on their facilities and premises are opened wide day and night. Lights are always on, as is the music! They achieve incredible results in the milking industry by doing so! Unbelievable sight. Unbelievable culture.

The only downside was that I and two of our children developed allergies. Despite taking daily medication, our condition worsened. Tests revealed that Daniela had an extreme sensitivity to cow dander—over 1,000% above the norm!

Ironically, Daniela adored the farm.

She loved watching the newborn calves drink milk from bottles hanging on hooks—a heartwarming sight!

12. Where Do We Go From Here?

We began praying and asking God to change our situation and prepare for us a new place for us under the Sun. Our children's health became the decisive factor in this matter. The doctor warned us that if we do not make decision to move to a different location, recurring allergic bronchitis could develop into asthma. It sounded frightening. The owners were understanding and supportive of our decision to relocate to a new place. We had to step out of the comfort zone we had built for ourselves so far.

After six months of schooling at the local school, getting used to the teachers and classmates, we were ready to take our children and transfer them to new schools.

By this time we had stable jobs and a comfortable home, attended a Ukrainian-speaking church where we sang in the choir and participated in numerous concerts. We also made friends and acquaintances here.

Like a sandcastle washed away by waves, we began preparing for a fresh start—a new chapter in life.

After filling out an online application on the joint website of both the Red Cross and the Salvation Army, we waited for a response.

In the Netherlands, Ukrainian children were initially taught separately from local children. Dutch teachers conducted an experiment in several local schools by placing Ukrainian students in classes with Dutch students first.

However, it soon became clear that it was difficult for our children to attend such schools due to the language barrier.

It was decided to hire Ukrainian teachers, but there weren't enough of them. Tanya could have joined numerous schools where she would be hired in the spot.

However it involved challenges and hard work. Most of the time teachers had to teach multiple subjects, and classrooms contained children of different ages.

In neighboring Germany, for instance, due to lack of Ukrainian teachers, Ukrainian children were placed directly into classes with German students since their first day in a school.

After just a year of time, they could speak German fluently and could show incredible results.

We all were eventually amazed by how intelligent our children are!

In the Netherlands, our children were taking intensive language classes in their schools, and at the end of the year, they were taking a language test. Those who passed successfully joined the Dutch students.

The majority of the Ukrainian students succeeded to the amazement of Dutch teachers!

Ukrainians organized multiple Protestant churches in

spaces generously provided by Dutch churches. They were known as communication and support centers. Places, where you can make connections, listen and speak on your native language.

One of such churches was ours, located in the town of Waddinxveen, 15 meters below the sea level, with attendance varying from fifty to a hundred people at different times. A Sunday school was organized for children of various ages, along with youth gatherings and a choir in which we sang. Being here felt like stepping into Ukraine!

Twice a week, we had the chance to meet and spend time with our fellow countrymen, which felt like a breath of fresh air.

For some, it was an opportunity to simply open up after losing loved ones or coping with injuries, sustained by their dearest ones back in Ukraine. The sorrow and grief experienced in a foreign country often led to chronic depression and emotional exhaustion, which, in turn, could result in mental health challenges. It's terrible to meet multiple separated families under circumstance you can't change. Just few families remain wholesome. Children wanted to play with me, because they missed their loving daddies.

We were invited to participate in concerts, where we performed many songs in Ukrainian, shared stories about Ukraine with the Dutch, and collected donations to be sent to Ukraine along with assembled humanitarian aid.

We constantly heard about many projects being organized by caring volunteers with the support of local communities. We were able to join in collecting what was needed for Ukraine.

With the help of the locals, we witnessed over a hundred trucks being sent to Ukraine with essential supplies!

With posters and flyers in hand, we handed out leaflets at supermarket entrances and collected products and goods from generous people who placed their donations into banana boxes at the exit. It was a heartwarming experience to witness such acts of kindness from strangers with big hearts!

Finally, we received a response from the organization where we left a filled out application. We took part in online meeting with our new hosts, Marten and Barbara Koopman. All the furniture we owned then was one mattress! We were offered the opportunity to move to The Hague, close to the North Sea!

We were settled in a large, three-story house from 1853, located in the historical district of the city with high ceilings and enormous windows, right next to a school. Marten supplied us with the furniture we needed, giving us a table and chairs from his own family heritage! He hired a cargo van and for a couple of days helping us get together all we needed. Such a noble person deserve our deepest respect! He helped us with paperwork, schools and jobs. Daniela would eventually join the school nearby after joining first another school, due to enormous waiting line in the school in our neighborhood. Later we understood why.

It was probably the best school we had ever seen before. The school principal personally greeted the children and their parents every morning, giving them big huggs!

We persuaded them, that having a place in their school we would surprise them with mastering subjects and material in no time. We just knew Daniela's learning skills.

Within a year, Dutch students have to master one textbook. Daniela managed to complete four of those textbooks within just six months!

Daniel joined another school with numerous Ukrainian students. Dutch teachers were continually amazed at how intelligent Ukrainian children were! Soon after our students proved that they can exceed their expectations!

Our children began to settle down, make friends, celebrating birthdays and other holidays together.

One of our favourite celebrations here was King's Day.

His majesty King Willem-Alexander of the Netherlands would personally visit his residence in The Hague, traveling there in a royal carriage drawn by the king's horses to utter a speech.

Everyone dressed in orange, the national color of the Netherlands. The streets and squares of the city came alive with various shows and festivities, and the evening culminated in spectacular fireworks! We witnessed several parades, with hundreds of people participating in bright orange costumes, including cavalry and brass orchestras. Incredible atmosphere.

Before Christmas, they featured Sinterklaas, the Dutch version of Santa Claus. Even the police took part in school performance! The headmaster came forward and apologised to the festive crowd, explaining that unfortunately the key figure of celebration has been abducted. She reached her phone and called the police. Soon after, along with loud sirens and flashing lights, an abducted Sinterklaas, accompanied by the armed police officers, was delievered right to the door of the school, carring behind his back a sack full of gifts, to the astonished crowd combined of children and adults! Wow. What a show! You were simply losing a sense of reality.

We were amazed to watch the police at work the other day, assisting people and ensuring their safety.

One evening, David and I were riding our bikes with only one functioning light on each of our bikes. For some reason our batteries died and the both lights stopped working all at once. The police stopped us and let us know the rule.

After explaining us importance to keep the lights on, the police officer offered us a set of bike lights free of charge! We attached those to the bike, turned them on and continued our journey, being amazed by their approach to solve problems. How can one resist to obey the rules after such a humane attitude?

The Dutch exchange gifts and presents, hanging them on door handles of the people they liked. The streets were filled with joy, and the decorations were just gorgeous. The emotions were beyond incredible!

Attending services at The American Church of The Hague, we grew accustomed to worshiping in English and even tried singing in their choir. It is a very friendly church community full of wonderful people.

Our house was always full of guests. Someone would come to visit, while others were just leaving. We encouraged each other making our days brighter. Having anxiety and clamming up depresses your spirit. We organised and played soccer one day with the local youth and managed to win! Daniel and others scored several times. I played a goalkeeper. You better don't mess with Ukrainians!

We lived near the European Court of Human Rights, also known as the Peace Palace, a former prison where governors guilty of crimes against humanity await execution by hanging. On their emblem, you can see a twisted rope. Everyone of us dreamed of seeing the president of a country, guilty of the genocide of Ukrainians in these walls!

All our friends wanted to visit the place and take photos of themselves with the building on the background. In every language of the world, you can find here the word "PEACE."

Near us was the Madurodam miniature park, where the entire Netherlands is represented in tiny models. You look like a true giant here!

Just a ten-minute bike ride away, and you're at the sea!

Bagheera loved running alongside the bike, escorting us all the way to the sea and back, guarding us from local dogs on the beach! Yes, we are the family!

We enjoyed watching the sunset at Scheveningen Beach and treating ourselves to kibbeling at our favorite café on the pier!

Our boys were true heroes, after making a leap into the unknown, a bungee jump from a height of sixty meters above the sea! Unbelievable!

I would have never done so along with Tanya! To put that in perspective, a nine-story building is only 27 meters tall. Here was 60 meters! We marveled at our children's bravery, who agreed to the unimaginable!

One day the house owner scheduled an appointment to meet with us. He sounded somewhat nervous and concentrated. We fixed some treats and waited for the guests.

Usually visiting our place our hosts were inquiring about

our life, asking us if we needed any assistance. This time they were willing to talk with us without children presented. They were choosing carefully every word they were saying. Judging their face expressions we realised that they are here with a purpose to convey an important message. Tanya's intuition revealed her that probably we can stay no longer in the house!

So it happened. Soon the house would be occupied by other people. We needed to register for new accommodation right away. Familiar emotions have overwhelmed us again. Perfectly same feelings. You will never confuse them with anything else! We realized again that we are in a foreign country, relying exceptionally on God's mercy and the kindness of others!

Short notice- and you feel like walking on thin ice, cracking right beneath your feet. Soon after we would have to start it all over again right from scratch! New schools, new jobs. All from ground zero!

Prior to this day, our children had attended one four another five different schools, and I had already worked at three different jobs, each time getting used to it before having to quit due to the new move. Another chapter in the book of our life in The Hague was coming to an end.

Mentally were saying goodbye to the city we had learned to navigate sometimes without much reliance on a map, to the familiar faces, neighbors, and the house we had started to call our home. Once again we would be gazing into the unknown...

It was time to pack our bags, into which we would have to put our entire life! Another leap into the unknown. It feels like being uprooted once again, as if our roots were being plucked out of the earth. Like a displaced New Year tree.

All of this is happening without your consent, your will, regardless of how we feel or think.

This is what being a refugee feels like.

Uncertainty and instability.

13. A New Country?

The distribution point in the city of Utrecht, which had previously received and helped settle Ukrainians, was coming to an end and was on the verge of being disbanded, no longer offering assistance to newcomers.

We began searching for our place under the Sun.

We contacted our friends in Belgium and asking them good number of questions, considering this country as a possible place for our future. Part of Belgium speaks Dutch, while the other part speaks French.

Began considering again Genova, Italy, where Tanya's mother lives with her husband, as a potential home.

Two sisters of mine became refugees as well and live in Luxembourg. Should we also consider this country?

Another sister of mine lives in Halifax, Canada. Maybe Canada then? This place is known for the sinking of the infamous Titanic in 1912 not far from its shores. One has a cemetery here where people who drowned and froze in the icy water were buried. It is so painful to see the names of all the family members on the headstones, including babies, who were only a few months old at the time of their death. And the date of death was the same for them all. It reminded us of Ukraine, where russian missiles kill entire families, sharing the same house or apartment.

Or maybe Ireland, where Tanya's cousin and her family live near Dublin? It's another English-speaking country, that many Ukrainians have chosen after russian invasion.

We also considered Germany, where two of cousins of mine, Andriy and Vadym, live with their families. Five days a week they study German and take exams. With God's help, they organised a Ukrainian-language church, where Ukrainians can now meet for Christian fellowship. Nearby their place they have an ancient cathedral in Cologne, which was under construction for six hundred years straight and reaches a height of 157 meters, making it one of the tallest cathedrals in the world!

My son David, along with a team of like-minded people, started a Ukrainian-speaking Christian church community in The Hague.

They held several camps for children and youth, set up a Sunday school, and began other various ministries. After accomplishing all the tasks he definitely didn't want to leave it all behind and set out into the unknown! Here, he found work, friends, and people who became almost like family for him.

But you are not in the stage to choose. You are dependent on the circumstances. And you are shaped by circumstances instead of personal choice. Once again we all were outside of our comfort zone, no longer feeling any solid ground beneath our feet.

While we were in many places at once, we weren't truly in any of them!. Traveling somewhere, you can no longer say "I am going home!" Because there is no home! The place you were allowed to abide for a while is going to be taken away from you very soon.

We could only pray to God for help in finding our place! A well planned, stable life with a comfort zone became a history. Now we had to adjust to the challenges of our physical and emotional limits! The time we spent in our house was running out, and we couldn't stay there any longer.

Our suitcases were half-packed waited by the door. We knew nothing about our future destination, as much as the suitcases themselves!

The dorms where Ukrainians were staying had long since been full, while renting a place on our own would require a salary three times higher than the rent. Plus we had a pet with us.

It was like the words of a song: "Here I'm on stage again, in search of a new image!"

This was our third temporary residence in two years, and now we had to leave it behind.

Caught between a rock and a hard place, my family lost its peace and security, having zero confidence in tomorrow! For their good questions, we didn't have good answers!

Only God knows what a person feels like in such moments!

We started appreciating and supporting each other even more! We were reminding ourselves that home is neither walls or roof, but us ourselves, the family members!

This was especially evident in the relationship between the older and middle brothers, which had noticeably improved! We noticed this improvement and were very happy to see it, saying that there's no bad without good!

For us, this wasn't a survival theory. This was the daily practice of our life. The gap between theory and practice is huge indeed. Theory and practice are not the same. Not even close!

Couple of years ago my friend in Ukraine shared with me a story from his own life.

One day, he had to visit a dentist due to a nagging toothache. He had endured it until one day his cheek swelled up to an enormous size! There was no turning back. Instead of a simple tooth extraction, he was placed in a dental hospital for an examination, and later, surgery was scheduled.

Soon, a surgeon and a nurse worked on him in the operating room.

Since it was a local anesthetic, he told me he heard the crunching sound of the membrane bones inside his jaw breaking. I didn't even know such membranes existed!

I listened to every small detail of the story, which he shared generously, like drawing a picture right before my eyes. I had to say something. But I had no idea what I had to say. I felt very sorry for this guy.

Then I said something far cry from being very clever and later regretted. It was better to remain silent and just nod my head!

I told him that I understand him.

What he said in reply I will remember for the rest of my life. He said, "No, you don't understand. How can you understand me? You can't even imagine what I went through! You've never had anything of that sort! You have no idea what it feels like!"

That's the essence of theory and practice.

In driving school, they teach you all about the car. It obviously seems like not a big deal to sit behind the wheel and drive! Nothing special, right? You see many people do it every day around you. Here is the steering wheel, pedals, doors, and the engine. What can be easier than that?

But it's only when you sit behind the wheel and hit the road you begin to realize they didn't teach you anything, even close in that driving school!

Sharing prayer requests with our friends and telling them about our situation, one family from the United States agreed to fill out forms for us as part of a program called "United for Ukraine." The unique feature of this program was that it wasn't the government taking responsibility for us, as in the EU, but private individuals or organizations.

Our first sponsors were turned down for some reason, and we lost precious time. Other sponsors were allowed to fill out the forms and invite us. If approved, the waiting time could be anywhere from a few weeks to a few months long.

The house owner wanted to hear from us some concrete plans a long time ago, but instead, every time we only shrugged our shoulders. This went on and on for months!

I joked that if this continued on like that, we might have to set up a tent and live across from the local police station and fry sausages over an open fire! It reminded me of a story.

Once upon a time, a king conquered a city and imposed a tax on it. He sent his messenger to find out what the people were saying.

"The people are outraged and disheartened," the

messenger reported. "Raise the taxes higher!" commanded the king.

Some time later, the messenger went out on the same task again. "So, what are they saying now?" the king asked.

"They're crying and wailing," the messenger replied. "That means it's still not enough. Increase the taxes!" ordered the king.

Finally, the messenger brought back new information. "The people laugh and guffaw," he said.

"Excellent," said the king. "Leave the taxes at this level!"

Seems like we reached that high level now!

Uncertainty doesn't allow you to build any plans for the future. You go to bed and wake up without any idea of what the new day will bring. We learned to live one day at a time. In this timeframe trying your best not to think about yesterday or tomorrow. Enjoining the day of today is enough. Gathering in one of the rooms at night, sharing our feelings, trying to support and comfort each other. Why waste energy on something you can't change? Accept this fact and enjoy life as much as you can!

We even tried to convince the house owner to sign a contract with us and rent the place but were turned down, seemingly because in this case the contract couldn't be terminated for a year after signing. We dreamed to live entire year without being bothered or disturbed! Such a luxury is not included into the refugee package. The concept of a comfort zone no longer exists for you.

People around you are busy with their own life and necessities. The population of the city we lived in is 720,000 people, but it feels like you're all alone in the entire world! Truly besides God and your family, there's no one else indeed for you!

Some people from Ukraine were saying to us, "It's good for you to be there, abroad."

I always wanted to ask them, You really think so? Go ahead and try it! Come over! You will be surprised! More than you think or even imagine! One can never truly understand someone unless you filled their shoes. Theory and practice again.

The words you hear from people like "everything will be fine" only emphasize that things are not fine right now! This lesson is going to stay with us lifetime. You learn it a hard way by experience.

The lack of stability and uncertainty feel devastating and wears you down. You see people laugh and rejoice. You are staying close, watching them do it with zero emotions on your face, like a robot. What is going on with me? Where is happiness and satisfaction in your life? Even playing in the playground with Daniela you can't relax and stop thinking about your future. Your Temporary Protected Status only highlights your feelings.

Being an interpreter in Ukraine, I could see my schedule for the next six months or sometimes a year ahead of time! It greatly reduces the level of stress and anxiety about the future. This is what we got used to.

And enjoyed.

We prayed and prayed. God always hears our prayers. Even if you think He doesn't. The Sun doesn't disappear, just hiding above the clouds. There is time and place for everything and it doesn't matter what you feel about it.

No matter how long the night seems, morning will inevitably come!

14. Response

One day we had to attend a parent-teacher meeting at Daniela's school. Just in case, we brought a phone with live translation settings to understand at least a little bit.

But as it turned out, the teacher was far enough from us that our phone couldn't translate the conversation. We spent an hour and a half in the classroom, understanding only few simple words!

We really wished we were somewhere we wouldn't have a language barrier!! Speak and understand people. Please Lord!

And God must have heard our prayer.

While checking the mailbox, I noticed five envelopes written in English among the newspapers and ads. It was such a pleasant surprise to find something we could not only read but also understand!

Quickly opening the envelopes, we found a letter inside with our names on it. Boldly printed at the top was **"Travel Authorized."**

We have ninety days to cross the U.S. border!

We were so excited, and everyone wanted to jump for joy, which is exactly what we did! Remember, Daniela and I have our little tradition? When joy overflows, we hold hands and jump as high as we can!

Different feelings started to alternate in our minds. During the day, there was joy. But as night fell, fear and anxiety were taking over. We were taking another step into another unknown! You can never get used to it! It's like doing a blood test, or visiting your dentist. You can't relax and stop thinking about it.

Now we had to figure out how and where to buy flight tickets and plan our departure date.

We also started to think about how our loyal dog, Bagheera, would cope with the flight. My wife had brought her all the way from Ukraine a couple of months before.

In addition to her Ukrainian veterinarian passport, we decided to double her chances of avoiding any complications by getting her a European passport and vaccination to cross the border. We also had to figure out what to do with our family car, which had Ukrainian registration, and what the procedure would be for selling it outside Ukraine. Ninety days didn't seem like much time at all!

Only eighty-nine days left, and the clock was ticking...

15. Saying Goodbye

The Marriott Hotel, where I worked, threw a farewell party in my honor.

During my year working there, I held a good position and was responsible for the VIP clients department, called a Lounge Executive. My colleagues and I understood each other with half a word, half a glance. During my time there, the number of clients in my department doubled! When my clients heard I was from Ukraine, they were curious about what was happening in my country back home. Watching the news and knowing certain details, I got the impression, that in their minds, everything seemed like scattered puzzle pieces! I was trying to help them fit it all together as much as I could. I did my best to explain to them that this war had been started against us isn't just Ukraine's problem only. Ukraine is now like a dam holding back a massive flood of water, which, if it breaks, will affect everyone around, including Europe.

I had the honor of speaking with high-ranking military

officials. They wouldn't make any predictions but were closely observing the situation in Ukraine, playing it by ear, as they articulated it.

Once, the president of Ukraine, Volodymyr Zelensky, during a working visit to The Hague, stayed at our hotel! Since it was on a shift I wasn't working, so we missed each other.

Our head chef proudly told me later on he had the honor of making an omelet for our president!

We often had foreign guests staying at the hotel, since the embassies of all the countries in the world are located in The Hague.

Then came my last working day. Mentally, I was once again saying goodbye to another job of mine, and any hope for stability vanished when a newly hired employee was introduced to me who would soon be taking my place. My boss whispered in my ear that if my plans changed, they would be waiting for me with open arms!

On my way home, I passed by the russian embassy, where a long Ukrainian flag is displayed every morning!

Dutch volunteers bring it and protect it. Earlier, it had been torn down by the embassy staff. Sometimes, you could hear the Ukrainian anthem played there, reminding the terrorist country of the war in Ukraine.

Along the fence, there were many fresh flowers and a portrait of Alexei Navalny.

Once again, I thanked the volunteers and shook hands with like-minded people before heading home.

16. A Surprise with the Airline Tickets

We purchased plane tickets from the airline positioned itself as "pet friendly". For this reason we decided to fly with them, even though it charged some extra comparing to its competitors.

A couple of days, prior to the flight, we had to confirm our flight tickets. I gave them a call and found out that our flight was terminated. They apologised for cancellation of our flight and offered us the option to rebook with another airline. Rebooking the flight we were asked number of miscellaneous questions concerning our pet. They told us that the weight of our Bagheera exceeded the allowable limit. Therefore she couldn't be taken as either carry-on or checked baggage!

This news was a real blow and completely unexpected. We didn't think anything now could surprise us after everything we'd been through. But they managed to do it. Never say never!

We were in a state of despair and considered canceling

our tickets. However, the house owner, after speaking with them once more, advised us not to cancel all five tickets. Just David's. Together, they would figure out how to solve the occurred issue.

One stewardess, a guest of Marriott hotel, mentioned the dimensions of a soft-sided pet carrier that could fit under the airplane seat. "Put it on your shoulder at the airport and walk dancing-like, demonstrating light weight of your pet to everyone around!" she suggested. "The flight crew would be more concerned about the dimensions of the carrier than the weight of the animal! Don't worry."

"I will do that!" I said. "Easily. I promise."

It would have been a betrayal to leave Bagheera all by herself in the Netherlands! No way we would leave the country without our loyal family member! Sending her to Ukraine wasn't an option either.

By the way. Here is Bagheera's story, to shed some light on her and how she came into our lives.

One morning in Ukraine, my lovely ladies were waiting for a marshrutka (shared minibus) at the bus stop. We lived at the final bus stop.

Suddenly, out of the blue, they noticed a car had pulled over nearby. The door opened up and a small black puppy was suddenly kicked out onto the side of the road! It happened right before their eyes!

For people living in the dacha (country house) area nearby, it was common practice to dump animals they couldn't or didn't want to take with them home into their high-rise apartments to spend wintertime. As a result, we always had a lot of stray dogs and cats near our house.

When my ladies returned home from the city, they saw

the same puppy still sitting where it had been abandoned, waiting to be picked up, anxiously watched the passing cars! Later, we found out that it was a female dog.

We lived in a three-room apartment, and at that time, we already had a dog at home, a Toy Terrier named Julia.

One of our neighbors finds joy letting his Staffordshire Terrier loose to chase and kill stray dogs! Right in front of the people and little children! People preferred don't mess with him and turn a blind eye to what is happening. Not long before someone poisoned the stray dogs, killing our favourite animal who we fed.

We hate any type of animal violence and always did our best to prevent it! No one else here cared much about this problem except for us, which made us marvel even more.

I mean no one. We had to call the police on him several times, but somehow he always managed to avoid punishment and continued his disgraceful actions.

After short persuasion I agreed to let the puppy stay with us. Otherwise, she would have faced certain death. I surely didn't want that happen. We named her Bagheera because she was pitch black as night!

She reminded us of the heroine from the Tarzan cartoon, the black panther. Later, she grew long legs and began to look like an Arabian horse! A very lean, well-built body plus a loyal character.

After purchasing a pet carrier, we noticed that Bagheera's length and width were a perfect fit for it. Except she was just a bit too tall. Daniela, who adores animals, noticed that if Bagheera lay on her stomach, she takes up very little space! She just had long legs!

So, she took on the role of her personal trainer. Her task was to teach Bagheera to lie in the carrier and let her zip it up over her head. Needless to say, our dog was terrified of enclosed spaces!

Once, while visiting friends in Germany, we left her in a plastic transport crate for a short while. When we arrived back home, we saw Bagheera running on the roof of the flat roof of the house!

We couldn't believe our eyes when we saw the mangled door of the crate, which had been the path Bagheera took to freedom!

A true willful Ukrainian dog, for whom no obstacle exists!

17. The Flight

Finally, the long-awaited day for our flight arrived. The date was marked in red on the calendar! At first, we counted the months, then the weeks, the days, and finally the hours.

Wanting to leave the house clean and well-kept, we worked nonstop all night long before departure. We looked like those students who needed just one more night before exam!

David invited his friends from church to help us clock out. Maybe some of them would also need some things we couldn't take with us anyway? A big pile of clothes just wouldn't fit into our suitcases. Some of it was donated, and some was purchased. Some clothes we put on only ones and twice.

I will always remember this farewell party. Always.

I saw the way these children looked at each other, with tearing feeling of deep sadness and regret, not knowing if they would ever meet again. It just breaks your heart into smallest pieces watching that! This feeling is impossible to get used to! Never ever!

Under any circumstances!

Sometimes it feels like it's better not to make friends at all because one day you'll have to part with them! Your life becomes like a broken pot, pieced together from many small fragments! How many times have we gone through this already? Over and over again. Many times. All the same.

Someone once said that train stations, unlike any other places, are genuine witnesses to pure, true, heartfelt meetings and farewells!

David, along with his friends, worked hard to ensure that Ukrainians in The Hague had long-waited a Ukrainian-speaking church community! We all happily watched as it filled with children, youth, adults, all feeling like one big family!

The new pastor of the church called our family to the front at the end of our last Sunday service. We were standing there praying altogether for our uncertain future! We were witnesses to so much sincere words, tears, and hugs, many times over!

In moments like these, you are reminded that Ukrainians are an incredible nation indeed! No matter where they are, they come together and feel like one big family! For so much unites us! So much we have in common!

Quick to learn new skills, not allowing room for mistakes, they grow, becoming stronger and stronger, remaining wonderful and incredible people all in the same time!

In just a few hours David will be sitting on a plane, crossing the ocean, reflecting on what future awaiting him on the other continent...

After placing our suitcases in a taxi, I looked back at the house we had lived in until this moment. It was witnessing our joys and sorrows, our meetings as well as farewells.

Our "Home" picture was given to our host as a gesture of gratitude to let us live here and call this place our home for quite a while!

I glanced last time at the parking spot of our faithful iron family friend, silver Nissan Qashqai. With its Ukrainian license plate on, it silently bore witness to the war in Ukraine!

I had made an agreement with him, that he would faithfully serve another Ukrainian family from Chernihiv, just as it had served us, passing into their ownership.

He will always take a place in my heart!

In all the emotions and sentiments, I accidentally left our tickets and passports behind sitting on a shelf in the wardrobe!

So many times I thank God for my attentive and reliable spouse, holding my back again and again, thinking sometimes for both of us!

With European precision, we were taken to Schiphol Airport in Amsterdam. Now our former host, of now-former house, a very busy and businesslike person, was helping us with our suitcases today!

By the way he was the one who had ordered a taxi for us ahead of time, at his own expense. He was the one, who organized a farewell party for us a week before prior to this day! He was THE one.

Thank you wholeheartedly dearest Marten and Barbara for all you have done for us! Sincere appreciation to you! We will be forever grateful to this incredible couple for all the kindness they showed us by allowing us to live in their lovely house almost a year long.

Together with volunteer Jeanette, they truly demonstrated an abundance of love and care for us, filling out our outmost need for a dwelling place! May God bless them all for their goodness and compassionate hearts!

Each member of our family was allowed to have one 23-kilogram suitcase and one piece of carry-on luggage. You have to pack your entire life into it! You had to choose only the most valuable, precious, and sentimental things! We had to repack several times, trading items between what we wanted to take with us versus what we couldn't live without!

We weighed our suitcases time and again, sadly looking at the pile of things we were leaving behind.

Some things we had purchased here, some had been gifts. Most of them were staying behind! They were ours for only a short period of time!

Left behind were our favorite dishes, furniture, beds, plants, paintings, mirrors we bought to make our home cozy! Books, except for the Bible, were either given away or left behind, as well as shoes and winter outerwear that took up too much space!

Daniela really missed her aquariums! She is a passionate admirer of living nature!

At first, she asked us to buy her one fish. That's how she got her first fish, an Ancistrus with a strange crown-like beard on its head! She named him King. He would stick to the glass with his sucker mouth and stay like that for hours!

But, considering the fact he was lonely and sad, as Daniela educated us, she had to add a few more aquatic friends! Why not? They eat very little and don't take up much space at all!

We ended up with four aquariums, teeming with hundreds of baby guppies and ancistruses!

Daniela dreams of opening a pet store, where she will sell fish, animals, food for them and much more! She proved that at the age of nine, she can act like an adult! Regardless her bad allergies to pets like cats and especially guinea pigs.

Daniela's heart was breaking into small pieces at the thought that she was leaving her water friends behind and would never see them again!

Following the stewardess's instructions, I carried the bag with my pet tightly secured on my shoulder, looking forward, walking dancing-like style with a big smile on my face, demonstrating to everyone around that the weight of the animal was nonexistent!

People like that are appreciated at the airport, aren't they? Gotta earn a top grade in the stewardess's school! The rehearsal is over. Time for practice has just begun... Now!

I proudly led a caravan of people and luggage, with Bagheera on my shoulder, my suitcase and backpack behind me.

I looked like a cabbage head due to wearing extra clothes, which didn't fit in the suitcase! We didn't know exactly what exactly we were going to wear in Texas!

Not yet! Soon we will!

It seemed like Bagheera was afraid to even breathe,

staring nervously out of the mesh of the carrier. Having had a chance, she would have gladly shred the bag in pieces in no time!

The passport control officer turned out to be a young and pleasant lady. She carefully examined our passports and travel documents.

For some unknown reason, she halted and stared at Daniela's travel document while calling someone on the phone. We couldn't understand a word since they were speaking in Dutch. Marten was paying attention to what they were talking about. She seemed visibly nervous.

She noticed an error in the birth year on our daughter's document, which suddenly made her one year older. Daniela liked the mistake! She always wanted to be older! Now she had a proof for that! Check this out everybody! But she was the only one looking on the issue from that prospective.

The officer told me to put Bagheera on the scale. Throughout all of this, I was keeping a cheerful attitude! I was more than happy to do so!

By that time, fingers on my right hand, as well as my shoulder that had been carrying the weight of my dog, had taken on a bluish tint. But I was the only one who knew that.

Sometimes, it felt like I was carrying another dog of ours, our German Shepherd Elsa!

The airport worker first glanced at the scale, then looked away, then back squinted her eyes staring at the screen. She was downloading and processing information...It's okay. It takes time. I understand. Just do your best...

You could literally see numbers flashing in her eyes! I

wish that such moments were not allowed to be filmed! That video would have gotten millions of likes on TikTok!

The diet and intensive weight loss program for Bagheera didn't seem to impress her much. She was simply unaware of the fact that, prior to being here, in the airport, Bagheera had been running something like a marathon race behind a bicycle. All the way to the sea and back!

The officer looked at me first, then at her computer again, covering her eye with the palm of her hand, the one closest to Bagheera, whistling a happy tune, smiling, raising both eyebrows, and slightly shaking her head from side to side, singing the paperwork.

I guess that has been probably an international sign meaning

"I probably see nothing right now! Nope "

18. So, when, finally?

Daniela kept asking us this question time and again.
We were all just as eager to know the answer!
She was articulating it on behalf of all of us!
I told her she better prayed more and be happy she's not holding a bag with Bagheera on her shoulder!
It reminded me of joke.
A man who was paid in provisions for his work, was carrying home in a sack on foot. At first, he thought they underweighted him.
After walking a little further, he thought maybe they hadn't.
When he was getting home, he realized that he is probably the one who overweighted them!
I decided to get a breath of fresh air by putting the bag down. My bag seemed to come to life, rolling across the floor, catching a few side glances from the astonished people around us!
We approached the next checkpoint, where, after

handing over our passports and tickets, we noticed we were held up longer than other passengers ahead of us.

As the border officer processed our documents, it became clear he needed assistance. Calling over a colleague, they both examined our papers. What's going on over there behind the glass? Why is it taking so long? Minutes felt like an eternity.

Finally, they called over another colleague, who instructed us to follow him, take a sit and wait in a separate room. We sat on edge, holding our breath. Even Daniela and Bagheera were unusually quiet watching us, just as confused. Our eyes were filled with the same question: What are we doing here?

Finally, without any word of explanation, I was handed our documents and wished a pleasant flight. What exactly they were checking, we'll never know. That's just part of their job and responsibilities.

As we continued toward our departure gate, we spotted a display, showing the flight number for the Amsterdam-Houston flight.

It didn't take much convincing for me finally to take Bagheera off my shoulder and sit in an empty armchair in the waiting area! Man. Feels so good now.

As we looked around, Daniela noticed a huge saltwater aquarium with enormous fish! Guess who made there first?

The water was as clear as glass, and the large, flat fish with big bulging eyes swam in front of her face. Daniela's eyes were just as big when she looked at them from the other side!

She managed to spot fish with bright yellow and blue

coloring! Just like the Ukrainian flag! How did the airport know we'd be here? That's a very good question.

Gradually, we boarded the enormous Boeing 787 Dreamliner.

Stowing our backpacks in the overhead compartments, I placed the bag with my pet underneath the seat in front of me. Surprisingly, it was quite spacious, and there was still plenty of legroom for my feet!

Our seats were spread out across the cabin. Thankfully, the passenger sitting next to me, agreed to swap seats for my wife could sit next to me. We released our dog from her prison and she laid down under the seat, and remained there unnoticed during all the time of the flight! She refused even drink water. Poor thing. I am so sorry.

Nevertheless we were sitting next to each other now, with our eyes closed, holding hands and thanking God that everything was finally over! The boarding process had been successfully completed.

Ahead of us was a ten-hour flight over the Atlantic Ocean, taking us 8,000 kilometers away from the shores of Europe.

We had never been this far from home before...

19. A New Beginning

The plane's landing gear lifted off the runway. It brought us high into clear skies and accelerated our unknown reality. In our minds, we were saying goodbye:

To the yellow license plates with the inscription "NL" on them, surrounded by circle of blue stars! We were so much excited to see them two years ago for the first time!

To the he colorful windmills that raised water from one level to another

To the tall, friendly people, who were always in a rush on their bicycles!

To the cozy streets and alleys, paved with red sidewalk tiles

To Dutch language, which, even though you don't understand it, had become an integral part of their culture.

We will never forget how under any weather conditions we rode our bikes on their endless bike paths, the longest ones in entire Europe!

Guess what. There are road signs and traffic lights engineered for cyclists! Only here had we seen bicycles with a basket in front, carrying children inside of those. And not only!

Driving your bike here you couldn't help but feel like a celebrity on the red carpet!

We felt like Israelites, leaving behind their familiar reality and place of residence, walking across the Red Sea on the way to to another land, repeatedly witnessing miracles along the way! The only thing we knew for sure the that the Lord is going before us, for He Himself had opened these doors before us!

On the map, we saw the countries we were flying over: Ireland, Iceland, Canada, and four or five American states!

I was surprised to see that large number of plane's windows were covered most all the time! Personally, I would have loved to look down during the flight! Our seats were found in the middle of the cabin, far from the windows.

We studied the screen with the map in front of us intently. We noticed our plane started to reduce speed and descend for a landing.

Finally, the plane's landing gear touched down on the runway of George Bush Intercontinental Airport in Houston! We were overwhelmed by the feeling of being pioneers of new lands! It felt like we were inside of a strategy game, where a map opens up in front of you as you move!

What surprises and unexpected things does this land hold for us? What would catch our attention first?

We noticed a huge American flag inside of the airport and made a selfie with it!

We had the American flag in our house. But we've never seen on inside of the United States! Our American friends brought us an U.S. flag that had flown over the White House in Washington for a day long! It even came along with a certificate showing the date of the event.

We knew next to nothing about Texas, except for a few stories from my American friends and videos we watched in YouTube. Everything here was supposed to be bigger! We will see it in just a moment!

How much we love and adore life! How much we love to taste its flavour! Bit by bit. Thank you, Jesus, for being with us all the time! All glory belongs to You only! It's just awesome to be alive and enjoy living, having discoveries and adventures on the way!

Bagheera obediently sat in her bag, peeking out through the small windows on both sides of the carrier, like a kangaroo in its mother's pouch! She wasn't any less impressed than us, refusing to drink along the way! Breathing frequently, with her tongue sticking out, she was getting ready to see what was waiting for her ahead. After a while, we had our fingerprints taken and answered the airport officer's questions.

A search dog in an uniform sniffed something in one of our bags. An officer lady gave us a serious look. We were told to open it.

The trained dog looked both excited and curious, anticipating something down the road. This wasn't the first strange situation we had experienced in an airport today! The officer looked at us and then at her dog, intrigued.

We weren't worried much, as our things had already been thoroughly inspected in Amsterdam's airport.

Tanya bent down and opened the backpack. The dog

immediately dove into it, starting to... nibble on Bagheera's dry food!

Fortunately, Bagheera watched all this show going on through the windows of her bag! The dog forgot that her job was to check for something else then checking out her European colleagues' food supplies!

After the luggage and dog papers check, we were finally wished a good day and left the airport vicinities. Outside the airport, we noticed that our day had been extended by a full eight hours long! We were so curious to see what was around us beyond the airport borders look like.

What would be the first thing to catch our attention?

What would the roads and streets look like?

What kind of cars do people drive here?

What do the traffic lights look like, positioned beyond the intersection, on the opposite side of the lanes?

What color would the license plates be?

What were people wearing here in late March, and what the weather be like?

In our sleepy heads, everything was mixed together, filled with endless question marks , curiosity and anticipation!

I suddenly began to understand American visitors, who were coming to Ukraine. I finally realized how they must have felt like in another time zone, experiencing it now for myself!

Until now, we hadn't slept for two days in a row, and it was only noon! Plus additional eight hours bonus!

I smiled to myself because I thought of an amusing incident back from my work interpreter practicing.

One day I met an American preacher at the international airport in Kyiv. Our journey led to Kherson, 550 kilometers away, about seven hours by car. We arrived at our destination on Saturday evening, where the hosts had prepared a delicious dinner for us. He went to bed long after the midnight.

On Sunday, he was expected to preach at three church services, each two hours long.

The churches were quite far apart from each other. During the third service we were placed in the front row, facing about two hundred people who had come to church that day.

Guests are always the center of attention. It's always interesting to meet someone who crossed an ocean and speaks a different language.

Suddenly, I sensed the rhythmic breathing of the foreign preacher, whom I was about to interpret for in just a moment!

The pastor of the church didn't realize the fact that his guest was only physically present at the service! He began introducing him before giving him the floor. During this time, I discreetly nudged the preacher with my elbow, trying to bring him back to senses as subtly as possible!

I'll never forget his reaction after waking up. He turned his head toward me and looked at me intensely. It seemed like he was seeing me for the first time! Then he asked me a question I will never forget.

"Where am I?" he said

I said, "In church."

Then he asked me what he was doing here?

I replied, "Preaching!"

When?

I said, "Right now!"

After a few minutes, already standing behind the pulpit,

he remembered the main points of his last sermon. By the way the sermon was incredible and aspired!

After a long wait, our new hosts were thrilled to see us! We hadn't seen them in more than ten years! They were occasionally visiting Ukraine, as members of a choir, conducted by John and Shari Griffin. The entire repertoire was performed in our native language, easily understood and highly appreciated. Together we took part in various concerts, from rural House of Culture to the city Concert Halls, containing over seven hundred seats.

We remember those small costumes brought for our kids along with peanut butter by Tami and Dan. It was happening so year after year! Tami always carried a big plastic bucket, full of Double Bubble and Tootsie Rolls, followed by large groups of kids, escorted her all the time. Their daughter Hannah was loved and adored by everyone in Ukraine, not only by our kids. After a group photo at the airport, we loaded our luggage into both of their cars. Ahead of us was a one-and-a-half-hour journey to College Station, home of one of the largest universities in the world, famous Texas A&M! More than seventy thousand students study here simultaneously!

We could hardly believe we were about to see it soon with our own eyes! It was like a city within another city! Later on I would even be working here for a while!

We quickly realized that in Texas, everything was indeed bigger! Those pick up trucks around us were simply enormous! And they were everywhere!

In Europe, for instance, to park your vehicle, you first had to find a parking spot, then squeeze between two cars, showing off our parallel parking skills! One on a pick up truck would spend some big time to find a parking spot for such monsters like that!

The width of the roads left a lasting impression on us. The roads must have been engineered for those large pick up trucks! And other huge trucks with long noses! I got it!

I thought, why not add here an additional lane, made of the shoulder of the road? Lots of room available on the highways! Are those roads really made of a light gray concrete?

We were amazed by the variety of colorful wildflowers along the roadside! We had never seen so many wildflowers in a field before! The fields looked like as if they had been painted in multiple colours by a magical brush!

On the license plates, we saw the word "Texas." Daniel pointed out that the name "Texas" only differed by only one letter in our language! The rest of the letters look just the same! The background is white, just like it is in Ukraine!

After settling our luggage in the rooms of a large house in a sought after neighborhood with high ceilings and well-maintained interiors and exteriors, we saw a cake with a yellow-blue flag, sitting in the middle of the round table! Our hosts' mother, Bobbye, which is affectionately called here MeMaw, for many incredible qualities she owns, was celebrating her birthday on this day. March 23 coincided with the day of our arrival!

On the Dr. Pepper bottle, sitting right in front of me on the table, I also noticed the number **23**!

To our surprise, on May 23, 2024, Tanya and I would celebrate our **23rd** wedding anniversary! The house we are renting nowadays, also has the mysterious number **23**!

What a strange coincidence, we thought?

Numbers don't lie, someone added.

20. Is That for Real?

The next morning, we were already sitting in the church! We could not wait to see the churches from inside!

In the same time we did not want to repeat the story of the preacher in Kherson!

I had never seen so many churches anywhere in the world! We absolutely adore churches and everything associated with them!

First we noticed the great number of churches on the way and wondered , "How many people will attend the Sunday service?" We will find out in a couple of hours!

To our surprise on Sunday morning, we saw so many cars in the parking lots around the churches, that it seemed there was barely room for an apple to fall, as we say in Ukraine! Thank you Jesus!!

People, dressed in their Sunday best, entered the church buildings with their entire families. I've always enjoyed watching people walk to church!

We noticed two police officers inside of the church

building, armed with guns, wearing cowboy hats and boots! It looks like Texas!

Friendly Sunday school teachers joyfully greeted the children as they entered the Sunday school building.

Daniela spotted an aquarium with seawater. In an instant, she was standing in front of it, studying the fish. To her surprise, she spotted a yellow-and-blue fish in one! Simply incredible.

It took us a couple of months to receive our work permits and documents. Time seemed to stretch on forever!

We enrolled our children in new schools. This is already their eighth school straight in the past two years!

As we later learned, Europe has an eleven-year education system, while the U.S. has a twelve-year system. Therefore, at the start of the new school year, both of our children were moved up a grade, and Daniela was even transferred to a different school! Daniela's school emblem now features a wise owl, while Daniel's has a fast cougar.

Our clever and smart kids continue to amaze us and their teachers with their academic success and great results!

Recently, Daniela proudly shared her achievements in a sociology quiz among fifth-graders. She took first place with a score of 950 points! The second-place winner had 420 points. That is Daniela style!

All the subjects at her school are now taught in English, which is still a foreign language to our kids!

God blessed us with an unforgettable meeting with a Youth and Student pastor Brian Smith from the Christ Church in College Station. And its leaders, who showed us what true care and love for people look like in practice! And not just for the members of their church! Refugees like us were accepted and embraced in that loving community! We had never encountered such a friendly attitude from a pastor before!

A variety of services for all age groups are kindly offered here for anyone who wishes to participate. Thank you pastor Brian and Christ Church! Highly recommended. It's a place to be. May God reward you a hundredfold for your kindness!

Among the members of the church, God brought us together with two wonderful Ukrainian families, who honor their roots and history. Even though they've never been to Ukraine in their lives! Born in Canada, they have Ukrainian names and surnames. Pavlo, Myron, Mudryk—these names highlight their Ukrainian heritage. Incredible families! Be blessed and kept by the Lord!

I want to express sincere appreciation to the family of Jill and Jeremy Blest, and their sons Matthew and Johnny. They assisted our son David with accommodation and a place of work. You are gorgeous individuals, full of love and compassion! You're an example of how to love God wholeheartedly and your neighbour as yourself.

In College Station we had the opportunity to meet compassionate people and organizations with a pro-Ukrainian stance, who have been helping Ukraine in every possible way! Whose house is adorned with a Ukrainian flag and a sign **"STAND WITH UKRAINE"**

I would love to especially mention Mr. Jerry Fox, who has been organizing various events for those interested, since the start of the russian invasion. These events provide detailed information from the front lines and keep its finger on the pulse! On behalf of all Ukrainians please accept our gratitude!

We listened to incredible stories from Michael, a former American military medic, who is now on the front lines, helping Ukrainian surgeons apply life-saving tourniquets and perform surgeries in field hospitals. Altogether we participated in collecting components for the tourniquets, to help our precious soldiers who have just lost limbs! While assembling those kits, we prayed over each set we touched!

While translating postcards with heartfelt wishes from our American friends, sponsors, and benefactors, we prayed together for victory over the enemy, asking God to protect our homeland and give us the long-awaited peace in Ukraine!

Only together, each participating from his side and according to his ability, we can bring the victory of Ukraine closer!

And we believe that victory is already just around the corner!

We personally express our deepest respect and gratitude to all volunteers, sponsors, benefactors, heads of various organizations, and all those who care about Ukraine's fate and territorial integrity!

Sincere gratitude for your interest and support of Ukraine! Let's stand for Ukraine today and see one beautiful and powerful tomorrow!

A low bow to you!
Glory to Ukraine!
Glory to Jesus Christ!
Glory to the heroes!

To be continued

Our family - Pavlo, Tetiana, David, Daniel, Daniela

A dead traffic jam

A car ran over by the russian tank

Maternity hospital Adonis.
Kyiv-Zhytomyr highway

Lyceum 25 after direct bomb hit
Zhytomyr, Ukraine

Right by the totalled lyceum building stands a church building, fully intact
Zhytomyr, Ukraine

Constant blackouts look like this
Zhytomyr, Ukraine

Our lifebuoy, Nissan Qashgai

Bagheera. Our guard and loyal family member

Protesting against the war with Polish citizens
Krakow, Poland

Schindler's factory
Krakow, Poland

Matheus, our angel, who we trailed behind to the Netherlands

Kees and Tanya, who invited us to the Netherlands

House of Jan and Lies, the first family, who accommodated us
Hazerswoude Dorp, the Netherlands

Tanya noticed this birch tree behind our window after four months living in the house after she finally recovered after shock
Hazerswoude Dorp, the Netherlands

Our hero Nissan Qashqai, holder of the Ukrainian license plates, a silent witness of the war, parked by our apartment in the Hague

Marten, Barbara, Janette with our family
The Hague, the Netherlands

Peace Palace
The Hague, the Netherlands

Madurodam
The Hague, the Netherlands

russian embassy
The Hague, the Netherlands

Telling the world about genocide
The Hague, the Netherlands

The real Dutch girl

Daniela inside of the milk farm

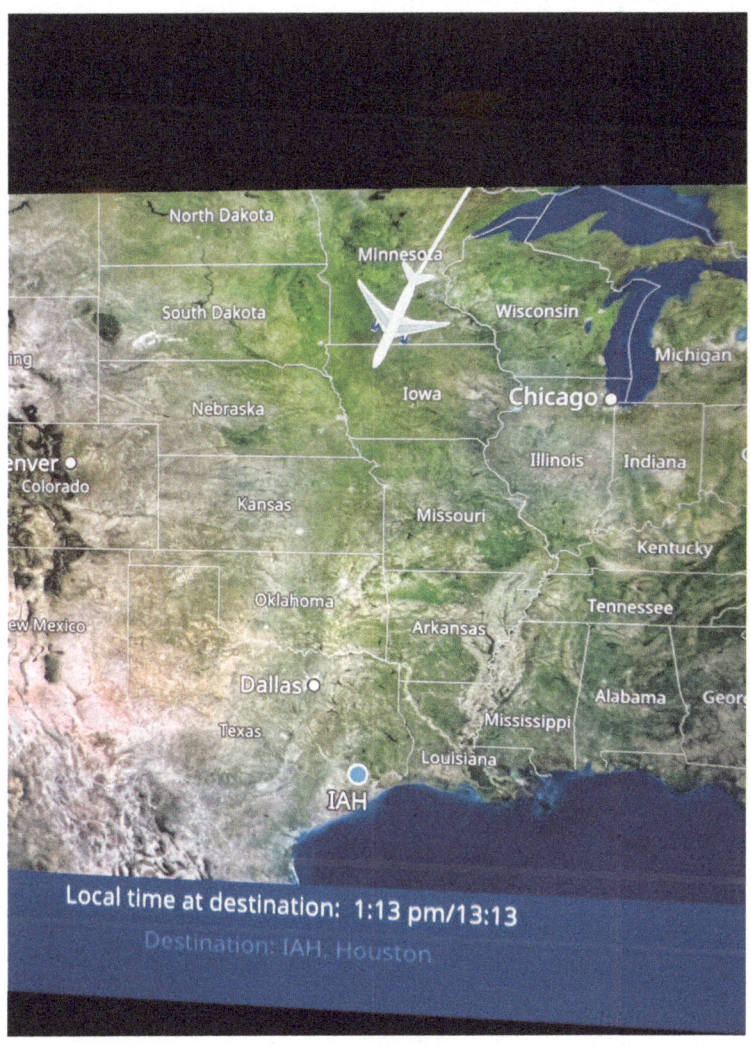

Our flight to Houston, Texas

Dan and Tami Stagg with our family
College Station, Texas

Trauma kits assembly
College Station, Texas

Trauma kits went along with cards containing wishes to our soldiers both in English and Ukrainian languages

Precious patrons, sponsors, supporters and volunteers, who stand with Ukraine

Made in the USA
Coppell, TX
24 April 2025

48643007R00085